Bonita Open Solution 5.x Essentials

Model simple-to-complex business workflow processes with Bonita Open Solution

Rohit Bhat

BIRMINGHAM - MUMBAI

Bonita Open Solution 5.x Essentials

Copyright © 2013 Packt Publishing

All rights reserved. No part of this book may be reproduced, stored in a retrieval system, or transmitted in any form or by any means, without the prior written permission of the publisher, except in the case of brief quotations embedded in critical articles or reviews.

Every effort has been made in the preparation of this book to ensure the accuracy of the information presented. However, the information contained in this book is sold without warranty, either express or implied. Neither the author, nor Packt Publishing, and its dealers and distributors will be held liable for any damages caused or alleged to be caused directly or indirectly by this book.

Packt Publishing has endeavored to provide trademark information about all of the companies and products mentioned in this book by the appropriate use of capitals. However, Packt Publishing cannot guarantee the accuracy of this information.

First published: November 2013

Production Reference: 1081113

Published by Packt Publishing Ltd.
Livery Place
35 Livery Street
Birmingham B3 2PB, UK.

ISBN 978-1-78216-708-2

www.packtpub.com

Cover Image by Suresh Mogre (suresh.mogre.99@gmail.com)

Credits

Author
Rohit Bhat

Reviewers
Giacomo Aceto
Roger Carhuatocto
Sebastien Prunier

Acquisition Editor
Vinay Argekar

Commissioning Editor
Amit Ghodake

Technical Editor
Iram Malik

Project Coordinator
Joel Goveya

Proofreader
Lawrence A. Herman

Indexer
Mariammal Chettiyar

Production Coordinator
Manu Joseph

Cover Work
Manu Joseph

About the Author

Rohit Bhat is a Computer Science graduate from BITS Pilani, India and is currently working as a Software Specialist in Opera Solutions. He has done projects in a variety of fields of technology encompassing Data Mining, Android Apps, Open CV, Swarm Intelligence, Workflow Automation, and Video Conferencing. He has been extensively using Bonita Open Solution for Workflow Automation and Business Process Modeling for a number of clients for his company.

You might find him surfing the Internet for any kind of knowledge and news, or plonked on his bed with a book in his hands. He loves to keep himself abreast of the latest technology and is a gadget freak. He is always ready for a discussion about any topic under the sun. He has a myriad interest in business, startups, entrepreneurship, finance, and current affairs. However, he is always excited to go on trips and tours, especially nature trails and trekking, with a camera around his neck.

Apart from reading, he likes to pen his thoughts and is a freelance blogger, too. He can play the keyboard but wishes he had more time to learn a new instrument. He loves to listen to psychedelic, slow, and alternative rock. You can say "Hi" to him at `mail@rohitbhat.com`.

This is his first book as an author. He is, however, a reviewer of Packt's *Android Application Programming with OpenCV*, published a couple of months ago.

> I'm deeply indebted to my mom, dad, and brother for being my constant motivators, and pillars of strength, and for providing encouragement throughout my life. I know they are even more excited about this book than I am, which says a lot about their enthusiasm! I'm extremely grateful to my friends for brainstorming with me on some ideas and my colleagues for helping me with the content of this book.
>
> I deeply thank Packt Publishing for providing me an opportunity to write this book. A huge thank you to the entire editorial team for their patience and invaluable help. I'm grateful to my reviewers for their honest feedback and suggestions.

About the Reviewers

Giacomo Aceto, born in 1983, studied Software Engineering at the University of Bologna in Italy. He completed his master thesis at the Uppsala University in Sweden (Informatics and Media Dept) and he worked on the finalization of a couple of publications. His main topic was AI: development of a Meta-interpreter for Defeasible Logic.

In his carrier, he dealt with European Research Projects, developing software and managing the software implementation process. In this domain, he has implemented Code Generators, Semantic Libraries, and interfaces among different kind of BPM engines and he has collaborated on the definition of an integration between BPM and IEM specifications. He published scientific papers at the following conference: *ICAIL*, *RuleML*, and *I-ESA*.

He is now working as an IT Project Manager in a company dealing with Facility Management and he keeps on working as a Quality Assurance Engineer (Test Process and Test Automation). Recently he has worked on the implementation of a Portfolio Project Management tool (CA Clarity) and he gained strong experience in terms of program and portfolio management.

Roger Carhuatocto has over 12 years of experience as an IT Consultant and Architect. He blends his experience in Computer Security with his passion for Open Source.

He has served in companies, such as Safelayer, Hewlett-Packard (Spain), and Thales Group (Spain), and has provided consulting services to PDVSA (Venezuela), Saraiva (Brasil), United Nations Office (Geneva), and so on. He has been involved in big projects related to e-ID Card, Identity Management, and big Business Applications based on Liferay Portal, Alfresco ECM, Bonita BPM, WSO2 ESB, and WSO2 Identity Server in Spain and Latam. Now he is a part of his own business initiative called Chakray Consulting, which offers high-level consulting services to build mission critical systems using Open Source.

www.PacktPub.com

Support files, eBooks, discount offers and more

You might want to visit www.PacktPub.com for support files and downloads related to your book.

Did you know that Packt offers eBook versions of every book published, with PDF and ePub files available? You can upgrade to the eBook version at www.PacktPub.com and as a print book customer, you are entitled to a discount on the eBook copy. Get in touch with us at service@packtpub.com for more details.

At www.PacktPub.com, you can also read a collection of free technical articles, sign up for a range of free newsletters and receive exclusive discounts and offers on Packt books and eBooks.

http://PacktLib.PacktPub.com

Do you need instant solutions to your IT questions? PacktLib is Packt's online digital book library. Here, you can access, read and search across Packt's entire library of books.

Why Subscribe?

- Fully searchable across every book published by Packt
- Copy and paste, print and bookmark content
- On demand and accessible via web browser

Free Access for Packt account holders

If you have an account with Packt at www.PacktPub.com, you can use this to access PacktLib today and view nine entirely free books. Simply use your login credentials for immediate access.

Table of Contents

Preface	**1**
Chapter 1: Installing and Getting Started with Bonita	**7**
Downloading, installing, and launching Bonita Open Solution	**8**
Creating a process	**8**
Creating a human task	10
The text variable	11
Running a process	11
The user inbox	13
The process history	15
Labels	16
Dashboard	17
The admin view	17
Summary	**19**
Chapter 2: Variable Types and Scope	**21**
Pool variables versus step variables	**21**
The text variable	**22**
The Boolean variable	**24**
The integer variable	**24**
The float variable	**24**
The date variable	**24**
The attachment variable	**25**
The Java variable	**26**
Summary	**28**

Table of Contents

Chapter 3: Creating and Customizing Web Forms — 29
Input and output widgets in Bonita — 29
- Buttons — 30
- The Select widget — 32
- The Radio widget — 32
- The date-picker widget — 33
- Variables required for the widget elements — 34
- The Image widget — 37
- The Message widget — 39

The Previous and Next buttons — 47
Summary — 50

Chapter 4: Conditions, Contingencies, and Transitions — 51
Conditional appearance of fields — 51
Contingency — 52
The JavaScript alternative to the contingency feature — 55
Defining conditions on transitions — 56
Gates — 57
Passing the message — 59
The call activity — 63
Multiinstantiation — 65
Summary — 70

Chapter 5: Adding Connectors — 71
Types of connectors in Bonita — 71
- Bonita connectors — 74
- The e-mail connector — 78
- The Drools connector — 80
- Database connectors — 83
- Groovy scripting — 85
- Other connectors — 85

Finalizing the web form data — 86
Summary — 88

Chapter 6: Configuring the Page Flow — 89
The inbox view — 90
Entry, view, and overview page flow — 92
User XP options in Studio — 94
Process status in User XP — 96
Externalizing forms — 96
Summary — 98

Chapter 7: Customizing Look and Feel — 99
- Customizing web forms — 99
- Changing Look'n'feel — 101
- Adding Resources to the workflow — 102
- Application Look'n'feel — 103
- User Experience Look'n'feel — 106
- Summary — 109

Appendix: Deploying Bonita on a Server — 111
- Downloading the Tomcat bundle — 111
- Exploring the Tomcat bundle — 112
- Starting and shutting Tomcat — 112
- Customizing database connections — 114
- Logfiles — 116
- Changing the configuration files — 117
- Bonita login page — 118
- Bonita API and adding users into the database — 119
- Summary — 123

Index — 125

Preface

This book is a hands-on introduction to Bonita Open Solution, a tool that makes creating workflow applications and modeling business processes a piece of cake. It is a practical guide, replete with examples, showcasing the ease-of-use of creating processes in Bonita Studio, and executing a workflow application using the powerful Bonita Execution Engine. We create a fully functional, practical workflow application that serves as an example of the potential of the tool. This book also introduces advanced functionality, leveraging Java, Groovy, and database concepts. It has a step-by-step approach, making it easy for you to learn by actually modeling a realistic process and creating an application. You will appreciate how Bonita Open Solution is a nifty tool for executing complex business processes and intricate workflows. It is a one stop solution for developing scalable applications with a great user management and easy deployment. This book has succinct tips and demonstrations that guide you as you follow along. By the end of this book, you will learn how to create workflow applications with ease by using the Bonita Open Solution.

What this book covers

Chapter 1, *Installing and Getting Started with Bonita*, starts off with installing the tool, Bonita Open Solution, and getting to know the various components of designing a workflow. It also shows an example of a simple process creation and getting it running. It finishes off by discussing the **Bonita User Experience** and administrative view options.

Chapter 2, *Variable Types and Scopes*, introduces the different variables that can be used in Bonita and discusses their scope. Instantiation and how different widgets use variables is also explored.

Chapter 3, *Creating and Customizing Web Forms*, explains the steps for creating a web form inside Bonita Studio by using the built-in widgets such as buttons, input boxes, messages, and many more. How the action buttons work is also explored in this chapter. In addition, conditional transitions from one step to the other have been introduced. By using all these elements, an example workflow application is initiated in this chapter.

Chapter 4, *Conditions, Contingencies, and Transitions*, covers the relation between different steps in the workflow. Message passing, call activity, and multi instantiation of a step are also discussed here. We show the JavaScript alternative to contingencies, too.

Chapter 5, *Adding Connectors*, looks at the various connector integration options available in Bonita Studio. We show how connectors can be used to fetch data into the workflow and how to export data, too. We have a close look at the Bonita inbuilt connectors, e-mail connectors, and database connectors, and also use them for the example application that we build. We get our example application almost functionally ready.

Chapter 6, *Configuring the Page Flow*, discusses the various options available for entry, view, and overview page flow. We discuss the various clickable features in the User XP and also have a look at the comments, attachments, and other sections that constitute the User XP. We also discuss the way to externalize web forms instead of creating them inside Bonita.

Chapter 7, *Customizing Look and Feel*, shows the various customization options in terms of the look and feel of the User XP and the web forms. We discuss the ways to edit and create a customized User XP and change the look of form elements.

Appendix, *Deploying Bonita on a Server*, details the steps that have to be followed to deploy BOS on a Tomcat server, changing the database connectors, and other configurations. It also explores the various Bonita APIs that are available and also has an example of a process using just APIs.

What you need for this book

The main software required to follow along with this book is Bonita Open Solution 5.10. There is a free version called the Community Edition and most features covered in this book can be used in the Community Edition. However, a few extra features that are available in the Subscription Pack (paid version) are also covered and workarounds have been suggested for the Community Edition. Bonita Open Solution has an inbuilt Groovy editor, due to which a separate IDE isn't required.

Who this book is for

If you're a software developer trying to create a workflow application or an analyst trying to model a business process, this book is the perfect companion to learn about Bonita Open Solution, an ideal tool for both purposes. You can use this tool to automate a lot of activities that had to be earlier done by mail or manually. With a rich web interface and excellent reporting features, the tool can be used for solving a plethora of problems, ranging from simple workflows to complex business logic. This book introduces Bonita Open Solution and takes the reader right into developing a workflow application using the tool.

Conventions

In this book, you will find a number of styles of text that distinguish between different kinds of information. Here are some examples of these styles, and an explanation of their meaning.

Code words in text, database table names, folder names, filenames, file extensions, pathnames, dummy URLs, user input, and Twitter handles are shown as follows: "Make sure that you have your JAVA_HOME environment variable set."

A block of code is set as follows:

```
import com.rohitbhat.examplepackage.TestClass;

  TestClass testObject = new TestClass();
testObject.setTestString("Default Test String");
```

New terms and **important words** are shown in bold. Words that you see on the screen, in menus or dialog boxes for example, appear in the text like this: "Click on **New Process** and Bonita opens a workflow with the predefined **Start1** and **Step1**."

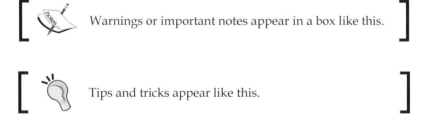

> Warnings or important notes appear in a box like this.

> Tips and tricks appear like this.

Reader feedback

Feedback from our readers is always welcome. Let us know what you think about this book—what you liked or may have disliked. Reader feedback is important for us to develop titles that you really get the most out of.

To send us general feedback, simply send an e-mail to `feedback@packtpub.com`, and mention the book title via the subject of your message.

If there is a topic that you have expertise in and you are interested in either writing or contributing to a book, see our author guide on www.packtpub.com/authors.

Customer support

Now that you are the proud owner of a Packt book, we have a number of things to help you to get the most from your purchase.

Errata

Although we have taken every care to ensure the accuracy of our content, mistakes do happen. If you find a mistake in one of our books—maybe a mistake in the text or the code—we would be grateful if you would report this to us. By doing so, you can save other readers from frustration and help us improve subsequent versions of this book. If you find any errata, please report them by visiting `http://www.packtpub.com/submit-errata`, selecting your book, clicking on the **errata submission form** link, and entering the details of your errata. Once your errata are verified, your submission will be accepted and the errata will be uploaded on our website, or added to any list of existing errata, under the Errata section of that title. Any existing errata can be viewed by selecting your title from `http://www.packtpub.com/support`.

Piracy

Piracy of copyright material on the Internet is an ongoing problem across all media. At Packt, we take the protection of our copyright and licenses very seriously. If you come across any illegal copies of our works, in any form, on the Internet, please provide us with the location address or website name immediately so that we can pursue a remedy.

Please contact us at copyright@packtpub.com with a link to the suspected pirated material.

We appreciate your help in protecting our authors, and our ability to bring you valuable content.

Questions

You can contact us at questions@packtpub.com if you are having a problem with any aspect of the book, and we will do our best to address it.

1
Installing and Getting Started with Bonita

Business Intelligence and business modeling has tremendous scope these days. It is of utmost importance to know, understand, and implement business logic that results in the success of any service or product. Modeling a business process and automating a workflow results in reduced time, effort, and various other benefits for all the parties involved. Bonita BPM is an open source BPM and workflow suite that is suited for creating high-tech workflows. It can be used for complex workflows, such as Supply Chain Management, Human Resources, Contract Management, and e-Government.

Hence, it is extremely useful to leverage this tool to better any existing workflow. A plethora of applications, across various domains, can be created quite easily and comprehensively using the Bonita Studio and Execution Engine. Let us get started with learning all about Bonita BPM.

This chapter serves as a quick start guide to Bonita. We would have a look at the following things:

- Installing Bonita Open Solution
- Creating a simple process
- Deploying a process

Installing and Getting Started with Bonita

Downloading, installing, and launching Bonita Open Solution

Bonita Open Solution consists of a studio for modelling processes, along with a powerful BPM and workflow engine. It contains an internal file-based database and a web platform for deploying web forms. Bonita Open Solution can be downloaded for Windows, Mac OS X, or any Linux system. You need to have JDK 1.6 for use with Bonita Open Solution 5.10. You can download JDK from the following link:

```
http://www.oracle.com/technetwork/java/javasebusiness/downloads/java-archive-downloads-javase6-419409.html
```

Make sure that you have your `JAVA_HOME` environment variable set. Bonita Open Solution is a portal where you can download the software, access some tutorials, and engage in discussions on forums. You will often find the forum a useful place for debugging any problem you might be facing.

1. To install Bonita Open Solution locally, download the BOS-5.10 zip file from the following link: `http://www.bonitasoft.com/products/download/other-versions-bos?field_download_version_tid=486`.
2. In this book, we will use the Windows version. Unzip the downloaded file to any target folder.
3. Launch the application by clicking on the file `BonitaStudio.exe`.

In this book, we will work with the free Community Edition of Bonita Open Solution. There are other paid versions available, such as the Teamwork, Efficiency, and Performance editions. You can have a look at the differences here:

```
http://www.bonitasoft.com/products/product-comparison
```

Now that we have downloaded Bonita Studio, let us get started with it. Here, we will have a look at creating a simple process in Bonita and getting it running.

Creating a process

In this section, we will find out how to create a simple process in Bonita Studio and deploy it.

1. First, launch Bonita Open Solution. At the start screen, you will have the option to create a new process or open an existing process, along with documentation and resources. For now, we will begin with creating a new process.

Chapter 1

2. Click on **New Process** and Bonita opens a workflow with the predefined **Start1** and **Step1**. The whiteboard is where we create our process and link various steps together. This view gives an overall picture of the workflow at a glance.

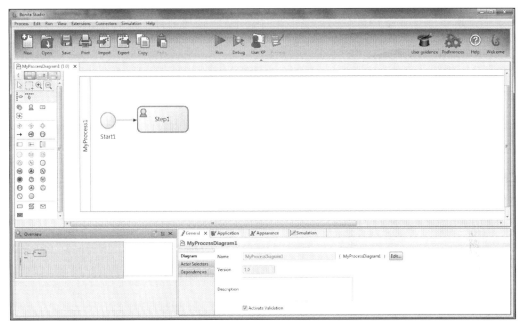

Figure 1.1: Overview of Bonita Studio

The black rectangle surrounding **Start1** and **Step1** is called the pool. Pools are akin to functions of any programming language, but can be run independently depending on their contents.

The left-hand panel is a palette consisting of various design elements, used to create steps, events, and triggers. The palette view can be changed to simple, detailed, or advanced depending on personal liking.

The bottom-left hand panel is an overview of the entire workflow and also has a search option in the tree view of all the processes and steps.

The bottom-right panel, dubbed the detail panel, contains the properties and data to define the processes, customize the appearance of the forms, and has options for defining dependencies and connectors. In addition, individual tasks and user forms can also be created and simulated from this panel.

As it is always a good practice to name all steps and variables according to their needs rather than the default names, let us get down to that first.

3. Click on the pool and click on the **Edit...** button next to the **Name** to change the name of the pool. Let us call this Demo. The version number is useful in case we want to create different versions of the same pool.
4. Next, click on the **Step1** process and change its name to Welcome. We will create a human task now.

Creating a human task

A human task is a process that is visible to the end user. A service task or an abstract task isn't visible to the user. Follow the given steps for creating a human task:

1. Click on the human task icon from the palette and drag it to the whiteboard, placing it next to the Welcome step. Change its name to Exit. You will find a red cross at the top-right corner of the step. This is due to the fact that an actor hasn't been defined for this new step.
2. An actor is a user or a group of users who are allowed to perform that step. To define an actor for the Exit step, click on the **Actors** tab after selecting the step. Click on the **Choose...** button and the available option is the **Initiator**. The initiator is the user who has initiated this pool. But let us create a new user who performs the Exit step.
3. Click on **Cancel** and select **Create....** A dialog box opens up with a prompt to choose the type of actor selector. We will use the selector method already provided by Bonita. Hence, click on the arrow next to **Bonita** and choose **User List -- Enter individuals manually** option. This is a way of mentioning manually the users who are allowed to perform this task.
4. Choose a name for the list being created, for example ExitActors, and you can give an optional description in the description box.
5. After clicking on **Next**, enter the words jack, john in the **Names or variable** box. Click on **Finish**. The users jack and john are already present in Bonita by default. Now, only jack and john will be able to access the Exit step.

   Even though we have defined the **Exit** step, it is not connected to the **Welcome** step yet. We do this by defining a transition from the **Welcome** step to the **Exit** step.

6. Click on the **Welcome** step. Thereafter, drag the arrow from the **Welcome** step to the **Exit** step. Thus, we have now connected the two steps and we have also defined the direction of transition.

7. Next, we need to end the workflow. For this, click on the **Exit** step and drag the circle icon at the bottom-right corner of the step towards its right. After you leave the mouse click, a box appears to choose the type of event. Click on the bottom most red icon, called Terminate End Event. A transition from the **Exit** step now appears to the Terminate End Event step.

> Alternatively, we could have dragged the Terminate End Event icon from the palette and placed it next to the **Exit** step. Then we would have had to create the transition from the **Exit** step to the Terminate End Event step.

The text variable

Next, let us create a simple text field that saves its value in a text variable. Select the pool and click on the **Data** tab. As we haven't defined any variables yet, this tab does not hold any values. On clicking on **Add...**, a dialog box opens up where we define the variable we want to create. A quick thing to notice is that you can name your variable even with spaces, but Bonita internally references it by the name that appears in the parentheses beneath the name you enter. Hence, it is a good practice to name the variables as you would do in a programming language, such as Java. Let us call this variable sampleText. The checkbox **Auto Generate Form** implies that this variable will be available in the entry page that is automatically generated by Bonita for each step. Leave the **Data type** as **Text**, because we want this to be a text variable. We can leave the **Default value** as blank. All the variables that are defined in the pool are initialized when the pool is launched. Hence, when the Demo pool is launched, the variable sampleText will be initialized to null as it is a Java String object.

We have thus created an extremely simple workflow with no web forms. Later, we will learn to create a fully-fledged application with web forms and business rules. We will now have a look at how to run this application that we have created and the elements of the UserXP window.

Running a process

Select the pool Demo and click on **Run** in the menu option. Here we have different options for running the application. Each pool is deployed as a web application and you can run individual instances of each pool. Each such instance is called a case in Bonita.

Installing and Getting Started with Bonita

Clicking on **Run** will deploy the Demo pool and start a case. Clicking on **Deploy Web Applications** will deploy all pools as processes, but will not instantiate any process. Proceed to click on **Run**.

The Web application launches in the default browser. The local web application is hosted on the jetty server that is integrated with Bonita. If you close the browser window, you can once again open up the User Experience by navigating to http://localhost:9090/bonita. This is the default port on which the User XP is launched. You will see a screen similar to the following screenshot:

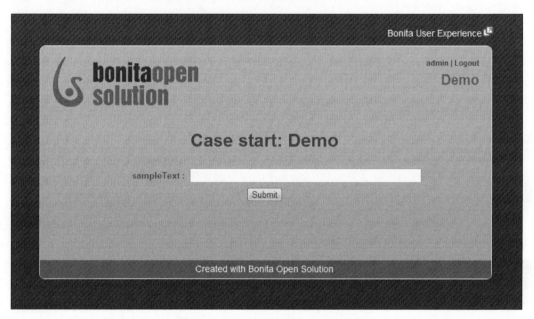

Figure 1.2: Launching the Web application

This form is the entry page form for the pool and we can initialize all the pool variables using this form. Type Hello World in the text area and click on **Submit**. This initializes the pool variable sampleText.

Now, the next screen that appears is the **Welcome** step. We have not created a web form for any of the steps. But Bonita creates an automatic form based on the number of variables that are relevant at that particular step. This is one of the good features of Bonita, as this form is updated whenever the number of variables changes. As sampleText is a pool variable, it will be shown in all the steps of the pool. Notice that the value of **sampleText:** is already initialized to Hello World, as we had defined it at the starting of the pool.

The **Welcome** step also contains the priority of that step, which can be changed in the step properties. At the top-right hand corner, we can see the user who is logged in and also the option to log out. By default, when an application is run, it is run via the admin user. Click on the **Submit** button. After the form is submitted successfully, a message appears that says that the form has been successfully submitted, and to continue we have to open our inbox.

The user inbox

The inbox can be opened by clicking on the **Bonita User Experience** link at the top-right hand corner of the form. The inbox is blank right now, as there are no cases waiting for the admin to be performed. Normally, all the cases that require the user to perform the next step appear in the inbox of the user. This inbox is like any normal inbox of a mailbox, with each line item in the inbox corresponding to a to-do list for the user. All the cases that are pending for some action by the user appear in the inbox and he can also see a list of tasks he has worked on in another tab.

We created the **Exit** step, too, but we had chosen its actors as jack and john. Hence, the Exit step will only be performed by either of the two users. Click on **Logout** at the top-right corner of the **Bonita User Experience** view.

Bonita opens up a login screen, where you can log in with the username jack or john. The password for the default users is bpm. After logging in, the inbox view of Jack is similar to the following screenshot:

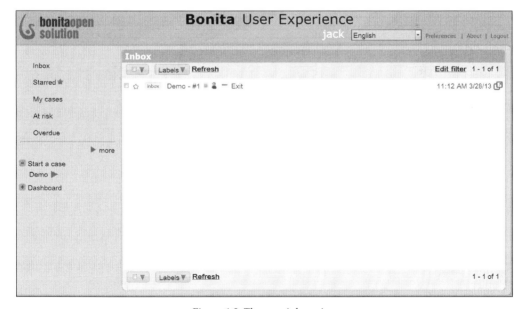

Figure 1.3: The user inbox view

Installing and Getting Started with Bonita

We can see that there is one item lying in Jack's inbox, which means that one case is waiting for him to take action on. If we look at the one row in the inbox, we can see that the process name is Demo, because that was the name of the pool in our workflow and the step name is **Exit**. Thus, Jack has sufficient information to garner that the Exit step in the Demo pool needs to be acted upon by him.

In the left hand panel, we can check out that there are various inbox options. In addition, it has the option to start a case, in this case, the case Demo. As we haven't specified who can start the case Demo, by default every user can start a new case. The first time we deployed the application, we created the case to be started by the admin user. Now, let's create a new case to be started by the user jack.

Click on Demo and we are greeted by the same entry page of the pool where we have to enter the value of **sampleText:**. Enter Original Text in the text field and click on **Submit**. The view that appears is similar to the following screenshot:

Figure 1.4: Expanding a row in the inbox of the User Experience

This view is obtained when you click on a particular row in the User Inbox view. In this case, the title of the row, along with the word Demo, has #2, which is the case number that Bonita assigns by default to each and every instance of a particular process. As this is the second instance of Demo that we are creating, Bonita assigns the value 2 as the case number. Beneath that is the entry form that Bonita creates for each step by default. We can either view this form as it is in the inbox, or open up the form in a new window by clicking on the red rectangle beside the button **Assign to me**.

Let's see what happens if we change the text of **sampleText:**. Change the text from `Original Text` to `Modified Text` and click on **Submit**.

As jack is the actor for the `Exit` step, the `Exit` step for the second case pops up and the text of **sampleText:** is `Modified Text`. This is due to the fact that the variable `sampleText` is a pool variable and as it is changed in the **Welcome** step, it is reflected in the subsequent steps too. Before filling in any form, click on the **Inbox** tab on the left-hand panel.

The inbox now contains two items, both on the **Exit** step, one with case number 1 and the other with case number 2. The items in the inbox are arranged according to a normal mailbox with the most recent item appearing at the top. Let us complete the two items that are pending in jack's inbox.

Click on the red rectangle in the row corresponding to case 1. This opens the form in a new window. The value of **sampleText:** is `Hello World` in this case. Click on **Submit** to submit the form. A confirmation message appears informing us that the form has been submitted. You can go back to the inbox by clicking on the link **Bonita User Experience** at the top-right corner of the window. Now, the inbox shows only one item as we have successfully completed the first item. For this item, change the value of **sampleText:** to `Modified Again` and click on the **Submit** button of the form and return back to the inbox.

The process history

We can have a look at the history of a process, which details the users who modified the process at each step and the value of all the variables at each and every step. Let us look at the process history of the second case we created. To bring up that particular case, click on the **My cases** tab on the left hand panel. The central pane is still blank. This is due to the fact that only open cases are shown at the moment. The user jack has no open cases at present as he has completed all the cases that were waiting for him to perform some action. Click on the drop down menu at the top-right corner of the User Experience and select **Show archived cases only**. Now, we can see the second case that we started. Notice the grey dot next to the case, which indicates that the particular case is archived. If the dot is green in color, it indicates that the case is still open. Click on the row corresponding to the second case.

Installing and Getting Started with Bonita

At the bottom of the screen, we can see a section called **Case overview**, and beneath that the `history` radio button is preselected. This is the complete history of the process `Demo`.

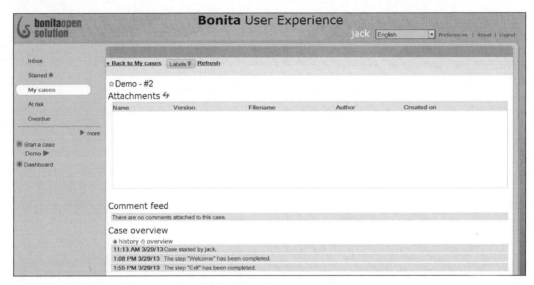

Figure 1.5: History of a process

It details who started the case and the timestamp when a particular step was completed. If we want to have a look at the value of the variables at each step, we need to click on each row of the history to display additional information. If we click on each row of the history one by one, we can check that the value of **sampleText:** has been changed from `Original Text` to `Modified Text` to `Modified Again`.

Labels

Labels can be applied to any of the inbox items for ease of use. These labels are similar to the labels in Gmail and work in the same way. Let us create a new label called `Demo`. Click on the arrow with the text **more** in the left hand panel. Select **New label** and enter the name `Demo` as the label name and click on **OK**. **Demo** now appears in the left hand panel. We can customize the properties of this label by clicking on the white box next to the label and selecting a different color for it. Now, let's create a new case by clicking on **Start a case**. Next, go to the **Inbox** tab. Select the checkbox next to the case and select **Labels** in the top bar of the inbox. Select **Demo** and click on **Apply**. We have labeled this case **Demo**. Now, if we have to filter multiple cases in the inbox, we can tag some of the inbox items with labels and we can access these cases by clicking on the label name in the left hand panel. We can also customize the visibility of these labels by clicking on **Manage labels**.

Chapter 1

Dashboard

By clicking on the **Dashboard** option, the user can look at the number of cases he has completed, the number of cases to do, and some other statistics in a graphical format.

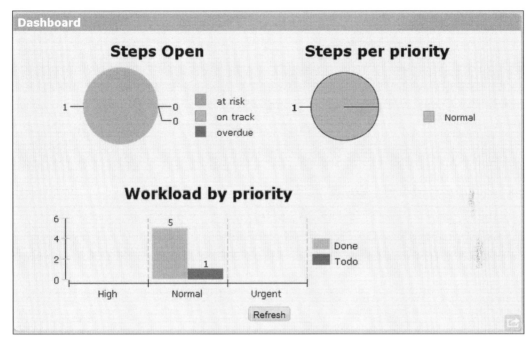

Figure 1.6: The Dashboard view

The admin view

The admin has special privileges, which gives him the ability of a super user for the application. Log in to the UserXP with the username `admin` and password `bpm`. The user view of the admin is the normal view as if the admin is a normal user. To check out the super user privileges of the admin, click on the **Administration** link at the top-right corner of the screen.

We can now see a variety of options that are available only to the admin. In the **Cases** subtab inside the **Processes** tab, the admin can view all the cases that have been started. In the previous section, when we were creating labels, we had created a new case. Open this case in the admin view and click on the **Submit** button at the **Welcome** step. We can still see the **Exit** step in the **Cases** tab even though the admin is not an actor for this step. The admin has the ability to complete the steps that he's not a part of.

If we click on the **Processes** tab, we find the description of all the processes that are currently installed. We can also install new processes from this section. In addition, if we click the checkbox next to the **Demo** process and click on the **More Actions** tab in the top menu bar, there are a variety of options here: **Open design** will open up the workflow as it was designed in the Bonita Studio, and **Delete all cases** will delete all the cases of this particular process. Then there are the other options of disabling the process, deleting it, and archiving it. Also, if we click on a particular process, it shows options for creating PDF templates, how the case number is indexed, and so on.

If we click on the **Users** subtab under the **Organization** tab, we can check out all the users that are currently present in the Bonita Workflow Engine. Here, we can also add users who have a role and belong to a particular group. Let us create a new user with the name su, having a new role called superuser. For adding a new user, we must first create the role. Hence, click on the **Roles** file menu and select **Add**. Create a role with the name superuser and label it SuperUser.

Go back to the **Users** file menu, click on the **Add** button, and fill in the **Username** and **Password** as su and bpm, respectively. Let us assign the **Manager** of this user as **admin**. Next, click on the **Member of** menu option. Here, we shall define the new role. Click on **Add** and we get a dialog box to choose the group and the role. Choose **platform** and **SuperUser**, respectively. Save the user.

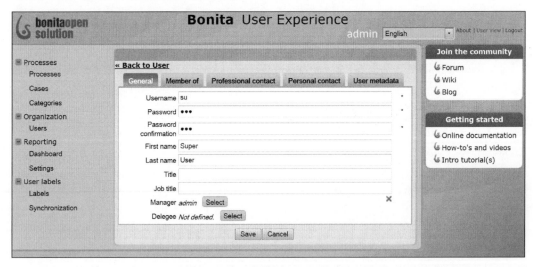

Figure 1.7: Adding users from administrative view

We can change the privileges of other users and also the privileges of a process under the **Privileges** tab. The **Privileges** tab is present only for the subscription version of Bonita Open Solution and is not present in the community edition.

Under the **Configuration** tab, click on the **Look'n'Feels** subtab. Here, we can see the default Bonitasoft theme applied. We can delete this theme and add our own theme, too.

There are some other options that can be explored using the admin view, some of which will be explained in later chapters.

Summary

We now have Bonita Open Solution up and running. We have created a process using various palette elements and learned how to run it. In addition, we have also seen the various User Experience options and explored the administrative view privileges. In the next chapter, we shall have a look at the various variables that can be defined in the Bonita Studio while creating a process.

2
Variable Types and Scope

There are many types of variables that can be used in Bonita Studio that are essential in creating processes. This chapter introduces all the variables available and also explores their scope.

Pool variables versus step variables

Bonita gives us the options to create two kinds of variables with regard to scope: pool variables and step variables. Pool variables are akin to global variables in any programming language and step variables correspond to the local variables of a function.

The type of variables, integers or text, are the same for both pool and step variables. Only their scope differs. For example, there might be an integer variable such as an ID number that might be required in all the steps of the workflow. We would have to make this a pool variable so that it can be accessed by all steps. On the other hand, one of the steps might have a field, called `name`, which might be required only at that step. Hence, it makes sense to make name a step variable that is accessible only by that step.

To define a pool variable, select the pool and click on the **Data** tab in the details panel. We can add the variables by clicking on the **Add...** button. Similarly, to define a step variable, click on any step and select the **Data** tab in the details panel. All the step variables will be listed here and new ones can be added, too.

Now, let us see the types of variables that we can create in Bonita Studio. All these variables can be created by clicking on the **Add...** button in the **Data** tab of the details panel.

The text variable

The text variable is used to hold text of all kinds in Bonita. Note that this variable is of the type string of Java, found in `java.lang.String`. The **Multiplicity** option is used to select whether the variable is a single string variable or an array of strings. We can also state the default value that this variable will take. If left blank, the variable will be initialized to null, the way Java Strings are initialized. This variable is used to store any kind of text value in Bonita.

The variable **List of Options...** contains a list of text variables that can be used in drop-down boxes or radio buttons. When we select the **List of Options...** as the data type, a box appears where we define the list that we want to populate. Let's name this list `Smartphones`. Click on the **Add...** button, type in `Apple`, and click on **OK**. Similarly, add more options. such as `Samsung`, `HTC`, and `Nokia`. We can also rearrange the list options by clicking on the **Up** and **Down** tabs. After we have created the list, we can click on **OK** to save the list. Note that the next time we want to add a variable, the option **Smartphones** also appears in the drop-down menu.

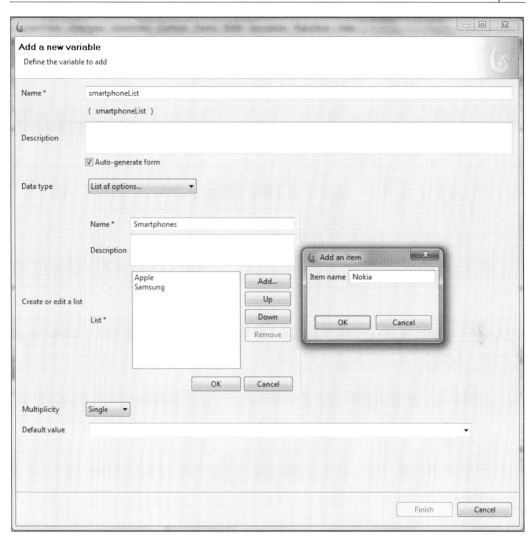

Figure 2.1: The List of Options variable

The Boolean variable

The Boolean variable holds Boolean values, that is, true or false, and is of the type Boolean of Java, found in the package `java.lang.Boolean`. Its multiplicity can be single or it can be an array of Boolean values. The default value of this variable, if left blank, is null.

The integer variable

Bonita Studio offers integer variables, but they are of the Java type Long (`java.lang.Long`). Be sure to initialize the integer value here, and if you want to use it for counting or keeping track of a sum of integer values, then give the default value as `0`.

> When using external connectors or Java code for evaluating the integer variable, beware that the type of the integer variable is not Integer but Long.

The float variable

In addition to the Integer variable, if we want to deal with decimal points and large numbers, Bonita offers the float variable, which is of the Java type Double (`java.lang.Double`). You can use the float variable for calculating money values, and so on.

The date variable

The date variable is used to store date values, for example, the date that the date-picker widget is in the Web application stores. It is of the Java type Date (`java.util.Date`). In addition, while defining the default value of this variable, we are given the option to choose it from a date picker that displays the date and time in a grid fashion.

Chapter 2

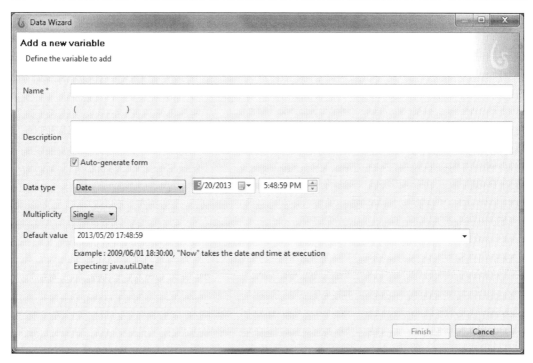

Figure 2.2: The date variable wizard

Also, the default value can be set to **Now**, which takes the date and time at execution. This feature is useful in most scenarios when we want to display the default date and time as the time when the end user comes across this variable.

The attachment variable

The attachment variable is used to store any file attachment in Bonita. As the attachment is internally stored in the database as **Binary Large Object** (**BLOB**), this gives the flexibility to store any kind of file attachment, regardless of the extension.

The maximum size of the attachment can be 15 MB. The attachment variable is primarily used in the file widget while creating web forms. Whenever the user clicks on any file object from his system, it is uploaded into the Bonita database and stored as an attachment `variable.XML Variable`.

[25]

Another way we can represent data in Bonita Studio is to use an XML variable to store data in the XML format. Relevant data can be represented in a concise way using XML. For creating this variable in Bonita, simply select the data type as **XML**. Here, we have to choose the XML namespace and element for the data. We can also add a new schema by importing an XSD file.

The Java variable

This variable is the most useful custom variable that Bonita provides. We have the ability to create Java classes and export them into a jar file from any IDE or Java command line. This jar file can be added to the classpath of Bonita. Thereafter, we can create a new Java object of the type of the class that we have created. Let us see how to do this:

1. Open up an IDE, such as IntelliJIdea or Eclipse. Create a new Java project and a package inside src. Here, we will name it com.rohitbhat.examplepackage. Inside this package, create a new class named TestClass. Enter the following code in it:

```java
public class TestClass {
  private String testString;
  private int testInt;

  public TestClass() {
    this.testString = "";
    this.testInt = 0;
  }

  public String getTestString() {
    return testString;
  }

  public void setTestString(String testString) {
    this.testString = testString;
  }

  public int getTestInt() {
    return testInt;
  }

  public void setTestInt(int testInt) {
    this.testInt = testInt;
  }
}
```

Chapter 2

2. Next, create a jar file from the compiled source code for this project. Name this `BonitaExample.jar`.

3. In Bonita Studio, click on the menu item **Extensions** and select **Add/Remove Jar Files**. Click on the **Add Jar...** button to add the `BonitaExample.jar` file. Click on **OK** thereafter.

4. Let us create a pool variable, called `testObject`, of the data type Java object. In the **Class** option, select **Browse...** and start typing `TestClass`. You will see a prompt with our custom class being suggested. Click on **OK**.

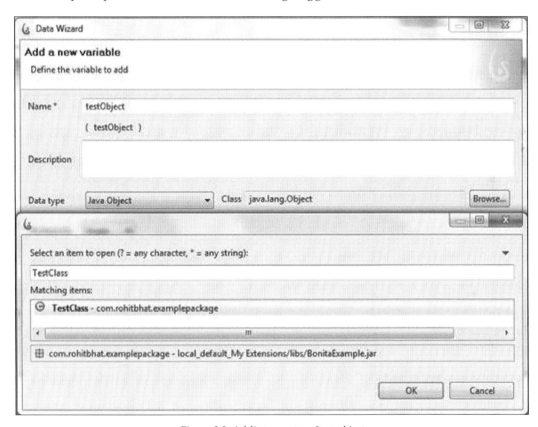

Figure 2.3: Adding a custom Java object

[27]

5. In the default value option, click on **Edit expression** to bring up the groovy editor. Here, we can define and manipulate our custom object. For example, enter the following code:

```
import com.rohitbhat.examplepackage.TestClass;

  TestClass testObject = new TestClass();
testObject.setTestString("Default Test String");
```

Thus, we can define our custom Java class and modify Java objects.

All the Java variables, coupled with custom Java methods, can be effectively used whichever way we want to. Inbuilt Java objects, such as `ArrayLists` and `PriorityQueue`, can also be defined in this Java variable and used inside Bonita Studio.

Summary

We have looked through the various types of variables that are available for use in Bonita Studio. We now also know how to initialize these different kinds of variables, and also which variable to use in a particular context. Any kind of information that has to be saved in the workflow can be saved in different kinds of variables. In the next chapter, we will use these variables to create web forms.

Creating and Customizing Web Forms

One of the highlights of Bonita Studio is the ability to design web forms in a simple and intuitive drag-and-drop interface. This takes care of most of the details while designing a web form. Also, in the description panel, we can easily define the data in the web form that we're interested in. Let us now create a new process, which incorporates many web forms. We will aim at creating a series of web forms for booking flight tickets by an agent. Let us look at the elements that such an application would have:

- A welcome page, where the user will be allowed to make a selection between booking a ticket and submitting a report
- For booking a flight ticket, the user has to enter his travel dates and so on
- Then he will have to choose the flight he wants from a list of flights
- Finally, he will be redirected to the payment page
- A confirmation e-mail will be sent to him after the successful payment
- He will also be able to submit a report instead of booking a ticket

Input and output widgets in Bonita

To create input and output widgets, follow the given steps:

1. Navigate to **Process** | **New** and rename the pool to `TicketPurchase`.
2. Rename the workflow to `TicketingWorkflow`.

3. Next, rename **Step1** to `Welcome`. This step will serve as the welcome page for the consumer. To create web forms for this step, click on the step and subsequently click on the **Application** tab in the properties panel.

4. Here, we have the ability to define the entry page form, which is the form that the user will see when he arrives at this step. The view pageform is how the user will access the history of the page. The confirmation page is the message that appears when the form has been submitted. We will now create a web form that the user would have to fill.

5. Click on the **Add...** button to add an entry pageflow. By default, the name of this page will be the name of the step.

6. Click on **Finish** and a blank web form opens up, along with the widget palette on the left-hand panel that contains all the widgets that can be added to a web form. There are various types of lists, text inputs, images, file upload widgets, buttons, tables, and HTML widgets.

Let us explore this section first. The blank canvas by default has a submit button, which is used to submit the form. For ease of inserting widgets, the canvas is divided into a number of grids. More grid spaces can be added or subtracted by clicking on the **+** and **-** buttons next to the grids.

The properties panel at the bottom-right corner contains the information related to the element we select. Right now, as the form is selected, it shows the properties of the form. Each form has a submit button that is used to submit the web form that is created. We can add buttons according to our needs.

Buttons

Let us start the process by adding a welcome screen form. In this form, we ask the user what he or she would like to do and, depending on the button clicked, we should navigate to the particular page.

1. Click on the button **Submit1** and change its name to `bookTickets` and its caption to `Book Tickets`. We will also add a welcome text on top of the screen.

2. Drag the widget **Text** and place it on the topmost grid of the form. In the general properties tab, change its name to `welcomeText` and uncheck the **Show label** check box. As this is just a welcome message, we do not require the label of the text box to be shown.

3. Similarly, in the **Data** tab, enter `Welcome`. We will modify the text later on.

This is a simple welcome screen that we have created in Bonita. Save the form. Let us now move on to another web form where the actual booking of tickets takes place.

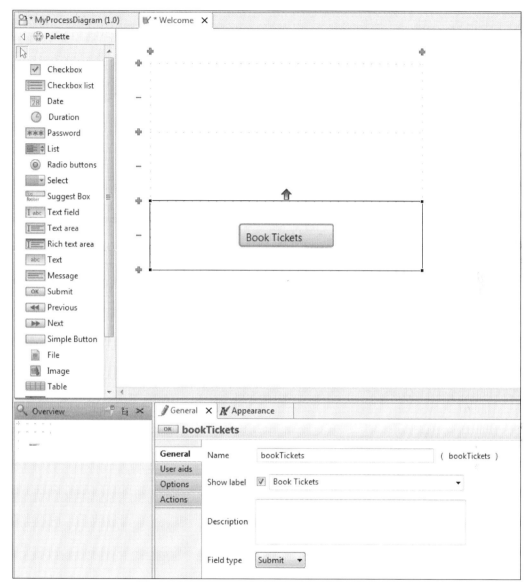

Figure 3.1: Adding a web form to the workflow

Go back to the process diagram. Let us create another step where we mention the dates and places for booking the flight tickets.

Creating and Customizing Web Forms

The Select widget

Let us get acquainted with the **Select** widget of Bonita and its applications.

1. Drag a human task next to the **Welcome** step and name it `Book Tickets`. Define the actor as the initiator.
2. Next, let us create a web form for this step. In the **Application** tab of this step, add a new form. Once the blank form opens up, we need to add widgets to this form.
3. The most important options while booking flight tickets are the **From** and **To** fields. In addition, we have to provide for dates, as well as the number of passengers. Let us have drop-down lists of cities for the **To** and **From** fields.
4. Drag a **Select** widget from the palette on to the form. Name the widget `From` and enter the same in the caption of the widget.
5. Next, we should have a **To** drop-down box, but it would be better to have it beside the **From** field. For this purpose, we have to expand the grids so as to have more space on the form. Click on the **+** button in the top-right corner to add another grid column in the form.
6. Insert another **Select** widget and name it `To`. Note that we have to populate the data for this select widget. The list of cities for both **From** and **To** would be the same. We just have to define this list once and fill it in as the data for both these fields.

The Radio widget

In addition to the **Select** widget, we will also explore the **Radio** widget here.

1. We need a radio button to choose between a single or round trip. It would be better to place this option above the two drop-down lists we just created. As we don't have space in the form to insert this radio button, let us create space by clicking on the **+** button in the top-left of the form. There are two buttons there, one for adding a column, another for adding a row. Click on the button that adds a row to the form.
2. Drag the **Radio buttons** widget from the palette to the form above our two list boxes. Name this widget `TripOptions` and uncheck the **Show Label** option. We aren't going to show any label for these radio buttons. We just need to select between **Single** and **Round** trip options.
3. Another thing to consider is that we should make the radio buttons options appear horizontally rather than vertically. For this purpose, click on the **Data** tab of the radio buttons widget and click on **Horizontal** in the **Items Alignment** option.

4. Also, we need this widget to expand over the two columns of our form. So, click on the arrow next to the radio buttons widget to expand it to the second column of the form.

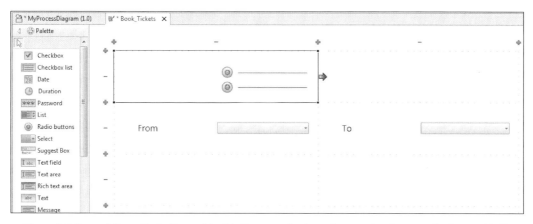

Figure 3.2: Expand the radio buttons widget to the second column by pressing the arrow button next to it.

The date-picker widget

The date picker widget is used for selecting the dates in a form. Let us include a couple of them in the form.

1. Next, we need two date pickers for the departure and the return trip. We shall place these two date pickers right beneath our two drop-down widgets. Drag a date widget from the palette to the form beneath the **From** drop-down widget. Name this `Depart` with the caption `Depart On`. Drag another date picker next to it and name it `Return` with the caption `Return On`.

2. We now need a drop-down menu to pick the number of passengers. Drag a **Select** widget and place it beneath the date pickers. Call it `Passengers`, with the same caption. Expand this widget so that it occupies both the columns in the form.

3. There is already a **Submit1** button on the form. We will rename this `Back`. Drag another **Submit** button from the palette and drop it next to the **Back** button. We will call this button `Submit`. Now, we have the outline of our web form, but we don't have the data to be populated on this form. Let's create variables for this purpose.

Creating and Customizing Web Forms

Variables required for the widget elements

We will create both pool variables and step variables for this form. The pool variables will be used in future steps, too.

1. Click on the step, go to the **Data** tab, and click on **Add...**. Let us create a variable called cities and define its type as **List of Options**. Here, we have to specify a list containing the cities. Name the list Cities and keep adding names to the list. Add the following names:
    - New York
    - London
    - Delhi
    - Tokyo

2. We also need another list of options for the **TripOptions** radio button that we have on the form. Let's create a new list of options step variable called TripOptions and populate it with the following data:

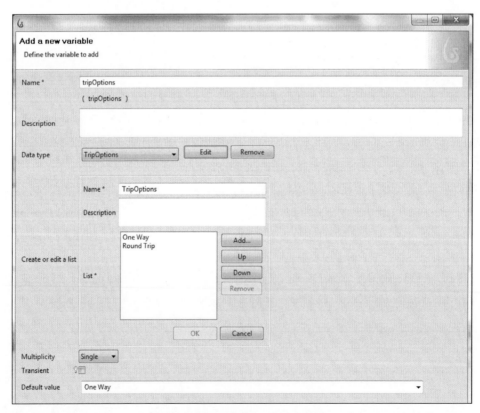

Figure 3.3: Trip Options data variable

Chapter 3

3. We would also need to create a list of numbers as the options for number of passengers. For this purpose, create another step variable called `passengerOptions` and include a list of options as 1,2, and 3 with 1 as the default option.

4. Next, we need to have date variables for our two dates. We can create pool variables because we have to save the date and use it in the later steps, too. Let's create two date objects with the names `departOn` and `returnOn`, with the default value as `Now`, which takes the date value when the workflow is launched.

5. Now that we have created this data, we need to save the field values in the **Book Tickets** web form into variables. For this purpose, we need to create pool variables. Click on the pool and add data. Create two text variables called from and to. We will save the value of the drop-down options in these two variables.

6. Next, we create text variables called `passengerNumber` and `oneWayReturn`.

7. We will now proceed to fill the data of the **Book Tickets** form. Click on the **Data** tab of the **tripOptions** widget on the form. Here, we have to fill in the values for **Available values**, **Initial value**, and also the place where we save the value selected or entered by the user. For this widget, there is a drop-down next to the available options pane where we can select either the pool or the step variables. We can also write a Groovy code that returns a list or a map as the available options.

8. For this purpose, we select **tripOptions** as the available option. The initial value can be filled with some value or left blank. If left blank, it defaults to the first element of the list. In the **Expression** tab, click on the check box **save to** and select **oneWayReturn** as the variable where the value will be stored.

9. Similarly, for the **From** drop-down option, select cities as the available option and save it to the variable `from`. Do the same for the **To** drop-down option.

10. For the date-picker widget, the initial value would be **departOn** and the **save to** value should also be **departOn**. Choose the **Display Format** option according to your need; for this example, let us choose **12/25/2009** as the display option. Similarly, fill in the data for the **departOn** widget.

Creating and Customizing Web Forms

11. For the passenger selection widget, fill in **passengerOptions** as the available value and save it to **passengerNumber**.

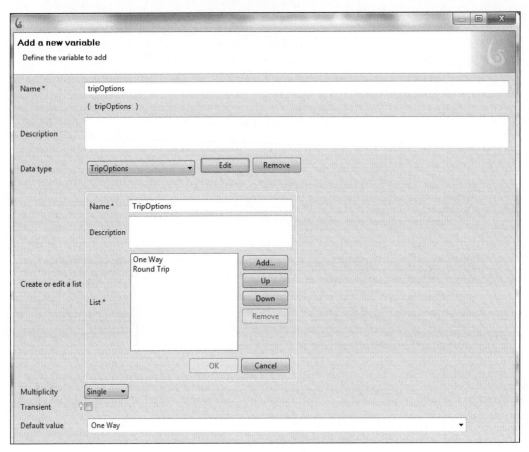

Figure 3.4: Filling in the data of the widgets

12. We will have a database connector at this step, which will fetch the available flights from the database and display it in the next step. We will define this connector later.

13. Let us create a new step called **ChooseFlight**, which will give the user options to choose a flight from. After creating the human step, create a web form for this particular step. This form is supposed to display the results of the available flights according to the information the user entered in the previous step. The data to be displayed is received from the database connector, which we will define later. Create a web form for this step by clicking on **Add...** in the **Applications** tab of this step.

14. Here in the form, we need to first display the information that was entered in the last form. For that, we create text widgets in the top row and populate the data as follows:

Figure 3.5: Displaying the top row widgets of the Choose Flight web form

15. Make sure that the date picker is set to **Read only**. You can do this by clicking on the date picker, navigating to the **Options** tab, and checking the check box for **Read only**.

16. Next, we want to display the results of the airlines available for the options we chose. For this reason, we will display the information about the airlines in a single row. We need to insert the widgets that display the information. Note that the data that we will be getting would be from the database in the form of a result set. We will populate the data for these widgets later when we write the connectors.

The Image widget

The **Image** widget in Bonita is used to display the images in Bonita forms. Let us include them in the form:

1. Let us have an image of the airline along with its name. Drag an **Image** widget and place it in the first column in the row beneath the widgets we already inserted. Name this widget `airline`. Leave the image label blank as of now.

2. By default, the label of an image is displayed to the left of the image. For pure aesthetic purposes, let us have the image label beneath the image. For this purpose, click on the **Appearance** tab of the widget and navigate to the **Label** subtab. Here you can find a radio button for the **Label position** option. Click on the **Below** option to make the label appear beneath the image.

3. Next, we would need to display the departure and arrival time of the flight. For this, drag two **Text** widgets and name them `Arrival` and `Departure`, respectively, with the corresponding labels.

Creating and Customizing Web Forms

4. Drag another **Text** widget and name this `Duration`. Then drag another **Text** widget and name it `Price`. Finally, insert a **Submit** button and call it `Book`.

 Note that if you run out of columns, you can always click on the plus button next to the grid lines to add more columns.

5. Change the default **Submit1** button to `Back`. Also, let us center this button. We can do this by dragging this button to the center of the grid, and then expanding it to occupy two grids, if needed. You can always change the way the buttons look as per your need. Here, we will first concentrate on the functionality.

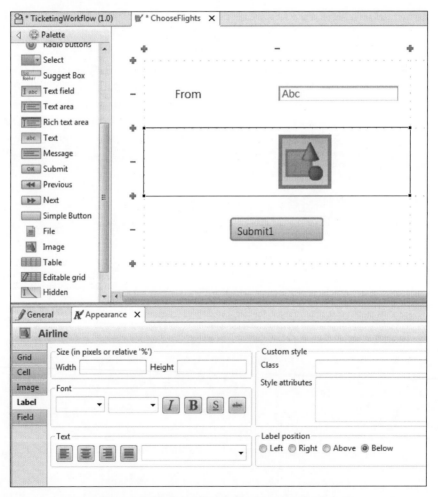

Figure 3.6: Changing the label position in an image

In the next form, we will proceed to the payment page, where the user would have to enter the payment details. We would also have to save the values displayed on the current form to show as a summary in the next page. For this, we would have to save the values of the variables that we display.

Let us create pool variables for this purpose:

1. Create the text variables called `departure`, `arrival`, and `duration`. Next, create another pool variable, called `price`, of type Integer and give it a default value as `0`. We can save the values of the flight information in these variables. We will do that once we have the result set from the database connector.

2. For now, let us proceed to the next step, which is the payment page. Here, the user has to enter his credit/debit card details. Drag a new human task from the palette and place it next to the **ChooseFlight** step. Name this step `Payment`.

3. Proceed to add a web form to this step. In this form, we first display the summary of the flight booked, and beneath that we ask the user to input details about his/her credit/debit card and passenger information.

The Message widget

A **Message** widget is used to display the information to the user.

1. Drag a **Message** widget to the top-left grid and name it `Summary`. Also, populate the data field with `Summary`.
2. Drag an **Image** widget beneath that, called `Airline`.
3. Next to it, drag two **Text** widgets, called `From` and `To`, with the data as the variables `from` and `to`, respectively.
4. Beneath the **Text** widget, drag a **Date** widget, and make its data `departOn`. Next to it, drag two **Text** widgets, called `Departure` and `Arrival`.

5. In the next row, we should have two **Text** widgets for `Duration` and `Price`. Make sure that the associated variables are selected in the **Data** tab of these widgets. These widgets should look like the following screenshot:

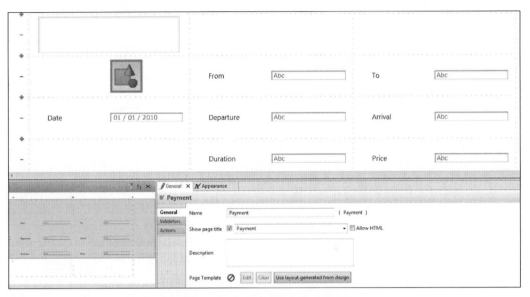

Figure 3.7: Widgets on the payment page

Let us detail the steps required for passenger info to be collected:

1. The maximum number of passengers that can be selected is three. So, we need three text fields for this purpose, but they should be conditional, that is, only as many widgets should appear as the number of passengers selected. For this purpose, we make use of the **Insert widget if** option. First, let us create these three text fields. Drag three **Text** fields and place them in the same row, called `Passenger1`, `Passenger2`, and `Passenger3`.

2. Click on the widget **Passenger2** and navigate to the **Options** tab. Here, check the box **Insert widget if** and in the drop-down next to it, click on **Edit expression....** Note that **Edit expression...** in all drop-downs opens up a Groovy editor, where you can write code.

3. For the **Insert widget if** option to work, the Groovy script should either return true or false. We have to make sure of that.

4. In the Groovy expression, let us write a piece of code that will evaluate to true or false. We need the widget **Passenger2** to be inserted only if the number of passengers is greater than one. We have saved the number of passengers in a text variable called `passengerNumber`.

Chapter 3

5. A simple Groovy code for this is as follows:
   ```
   Integer.parseInt(passengerNumber) > 1
   ```

   Let us have a quick look at the Groovy editor in Bonitasoft.

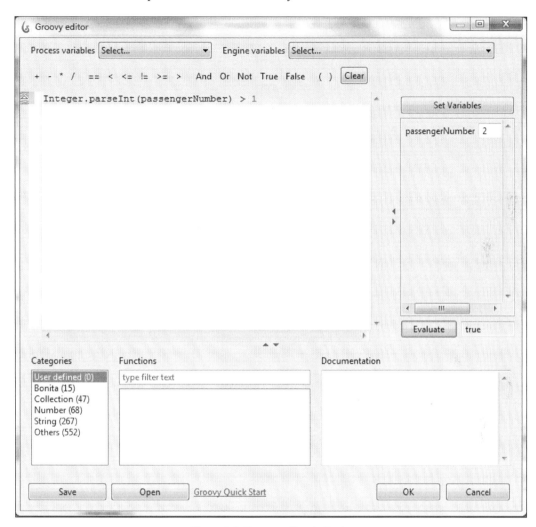

Figure 3.8: Groovy editor in Bonita

Creating and Customizing Web Forms

The top-left hand corner holds a drop-down box called **Process variables** where you can select the variables that you have defined that are applicable for this particular step. These contain the pool variables and the step variables. Just beside that, we have the **Engine variables** option, which are the variables that the Bonita engine assigns. We have `activityInstance`, `processDefinition`, `processInstance`, and other variables that are defined by the Bonita engine and are process and step related variables. It also contains the variable `loggedUser`, which is the username of the user who is currently logged into the application. If we click on the **Set Variables** button, we are given input fields where we can enter the value of variables and check for ourselves the result after the execution of this Groovy script.

If we enter 2 as the value of `passengerNumber` and click on evaluate, Groovy evaluates the script we have written and returns true. Similarly, we can evaluate whatever we have written in the particular script. This is useful while debugging our code.

6. Similarly, for **Passenger3**, we write the following Groovy code:

   `Integer.parseInt(passengerNumber) > 2`

   Another thing to notice in the Groovy script is that the Groovy editor is similar to Eclipse and other IDEs when it comes to code completion. You can press *Ctrl* + *Space* bar to invoke the code completion and make use of the available options.

7. Let us also create three pool text variables called `passenger1`, `passenger2`, and `passenger3`. Make sure that the passenger names entered in the widgets are saved to these variables. This can be done by clicking on the **Save to** check box in the **Data** tab of the widget and selecting the appropriate variable from the drop-down box.

8. At this point, we can revisit the first step, where we have a **welcome** box. Now, instead of just a plain welcome, we can have `welcome loggedUser` to make it more personal. Hence, open the **Welcome** web form and click on the **welcomeText** widget. In the data section, select **Edit expression...** in the drop-down menu and enter the following line:

   `"Welcome " + loggedUser`

9. Now, let us go back to the **Payment** web form and continue adding widgets.

10. Let us add a widget to capture the e-mail address entered by the user. Name this text field widget as `Email`. We have to check if the e-mail address entered by the user is syntactically correct. For this, we make use of the in-built e-mail validator provided by Bonita.

11. Click on the **Validators** tab and add a new validator. In the **Validator Type** drop-down box, choose **Mail**. Display the error message as `Please enter a valid email address`. This validator checks the presence of the @ and the . characters in the text entered by the user.

12. Create a pool text variable called `email` and save the value entered in this widget to this variable.

13. Add another message widget called `PaymentDetails` and enter the same in the data tab, too, with a space between the two words.

14. *In the next row, we enter the widgets for entering the credit/debit card details. Drag a **Text field** widget and* call it `CardDetails`. Here, we will have a validator on the field to check if the entered value is a number or not and if the length of the entered number is 16.

15. Click on the text field and go to the **Validators** tab. Here, click on **Add...** to add a validator.

16. From the drop-down for the **Validator Type**, choose **Long Integer Validator** because we have to validate whether the entered 16 characters are all numerals or not.

17. In the **Error Message** box, enter `Please enter only numerals`.

18. We also need to add another validator to check if the length of the entered input is 16 or not. For this purpose, add another validator and make its type **Length**. In the **Parameter** box, enter `16` and in the **Error message** box, enter the error message `Please enter a 16 digit card number`.

19. Now, we shall also make sure that the text field does not allow the user to enter more than 16 characters. For this purpose, click on the **Options** tab of the widget and in the **Html Attributes** option, enter the following:

    `maxlength="16"`

    This **Html Attributes** option makes sure that the user cannot even enter more than 16 characters in the text box.

20. Thereafter, we put in another **Text field** widget for the card holder's name. We also include a **Password** widget for entering the CVV number. For this widget, we enter `maxlength="3"` in the options box.

21. In the next row, we insert a **Message** widget called `ExpiryDate`. Next to it, we insert two **Text field** widgets, called `Month` and `Year`, which will have to be entered in MM and YYYY formats.

22. Finally, we move **Submit1** to the right-most column of the grid and name it `Pay`. We shall also add another **Submit** button and call it `Back`.

Creating and Customizing Web Forms

After these changes, the form will look like this:

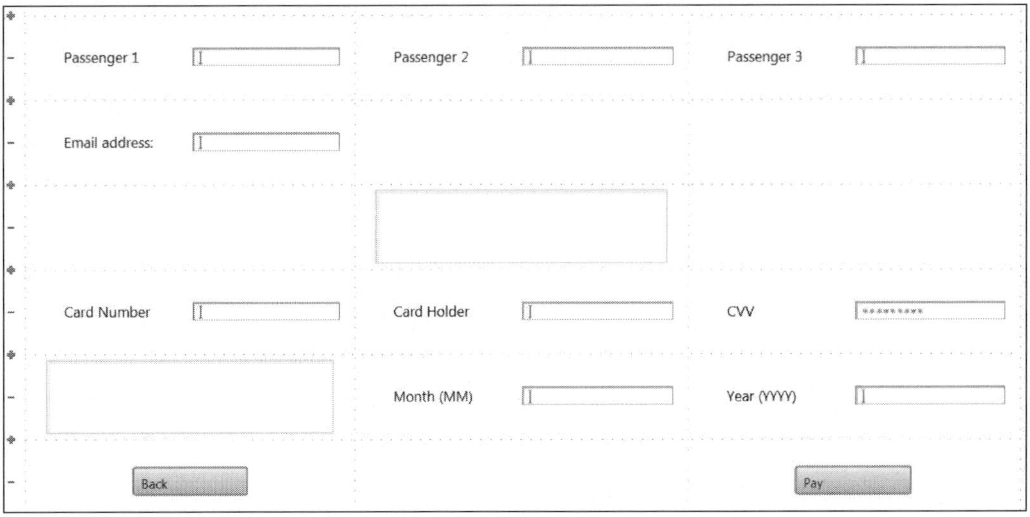

Figure 3.9: The Payment form

Now we have successfully made all the forms that we require for booking. Let us end this process by dragging an end step in the pool. Name this end step `EndTicketBooking`. Now, after the information has been submitted on this step, a confirmation message will appear. We can configure this confirmation by clicking on the step and, in the **Application** tab, clicking on the **Confirmation** subtab. Here, in the **Confirmation message** box, click on **Edit expression...** and enter the following code:

```
"Tickets have been booked. An email has been sent to " + email + " as confirmation."
```

This message appears once we submit the payment form.

Now, let us add another functionality to this workflow. On the welcome page, let us have a button called `SubmitReport` that will take the flight ticket agent to another page, where he would upload a file to submit a report. The next page, where the report would be viewed, should have a separate actor who would just be allowed to check out all the reports submitted to him.

For this purpose, let us first create roles:

1. Click on the **UserXP** button to launch the inbox view of the application. Click on the **Administration** view and go to the **Users** tab. Here, let us create two new roles called `flightagent` and `flightadmin`.

2. Next, we create users for these roles. Click on **Add** in the **Users** tab to create new users. Add a user called `jerry` with the password `jerry`. Make him a member of the `ticketagent` role. Thereafter, add another user called `tim` with the password `tim`. Make him the member of the `ticketadmin` role.

3. Let us now create the `SubmitReport` step. Drag a new step from the **welcome** page and name it `SubmitReport`. The actor of this step should be the `flightagent`. Let us create a new actor selector for this pool.

4. Click on the **Actors** tab of the step and select **Create...**. Here, we shall choose **User Role** as the type of actor selector. Name the actor selector `flight agent` role.

5. On the next page, select **flightagent** as the role name. Here, you can click on **Test Configuration** to check if the role returns any users. You will find that it returns jerry as the user. Click on **OK**.

6. Next, add initiator also as an actor for this role.

Figure 3.10: Actor selector in Bonita

7. Create a web form for this step. Here, we will just have an attachment widget through which the user will upload his report. First, drag a **Message** widget called `SubmitReportMessage` and, in the data section, click on **Edit expression...** and enter the following text:

   `"Hi " + loggedUser + " , please upload your report, click on the upload button, and then submit the form."`

8. Now, drag a **File** widget from the palette and place it beneath the message. We would also need a pool variable to store the attachment. For this, create a new pool variable of the type attachment. Let us name this attachment `report`. Now, as this is an attachment variable, it can hold any sort of file.

9. In the **SubmitReport** web page, click on the **File** widget and navigate to the **Data** section. There, check the **save to** check box and select **Report** from the drop-down menu.

10. Let us create a text widget for the user to write his comments. Drag a **Text area** widget called `Comments`. This is where the uploader would write his/her comments. Save the data in the new pool text variable called `comments`.

11. Now, the user has to upload the report and submit the form. Create another pool text variable called `reportSubmitter`. When the user clicks on **Submit**, let us save the logged user to the variable `reportSubmitter`.

12. Change the button **Submit1** to `Submit` and in the **Actions** tab of the button click on **Add...**.

13. In the expressions field, click on **Edit expression...** and enter `loggedUser` in the Groovy script. Note that `loggedUser` turns blue because it is a Bonita system variable.

14. In the **save to** field, select `reportSubmitter`. Also, create a back button. We will create the next step where any user of the `flightadmin` role would get this report and download it or review it for his/her purpose. He/she would also see the variable `reportSubmitter` so he would know who submitted the report.

15. Drag another step called `DownloadReport` as a transition from the `SubmitReport` step. Create a new actor selector for this step called `flightadminrole` and, in the **User list** box, enter `flightadmin`.

16. You can test the configuration to check if the user tim is returned. Next, create a new web form and drag a **Message** widget at the top of the form. Here, in the **Data** section, click on **Edit expression...** and enter the following code in the Groovy editor:

    `"The following report was submitted by " + reportSubmitter`

17. After that, we need to display the comments written by the uploader. Drag a **Text area** widget and name it `Comments`. Select **comments** as the initial value of this widget in the **Data** tab.

18. Also, in the **Options** tab, check the **Read only** option.

19. Next, drag a **File** widget on to the form. In the **Data** section of the widget, select **Report** as the initial value and select the check box **Download Only**. Thus, the flightadmin user will just be able to view this document that has been uploaded by the flightagent user.

Also, we need to make a change in the welcome screen. There, we had only one option for booking tickets. We have to add another button for submitting the report. To do so, follow the given steps:

1. Open the **Welcome** step and drag a **Submit** button widget on to the form. We will have to add another grid column to do that.
2. Place the **SubmitReport** button next to the **BookTickets** button. Also, expand **WelcomeText** so that it now occupies two grid columns.

The Previous and Next buttons

We have a **Next** and a **Previous** buttons on each form, but we have yet to configure these buttons. The way we can achieve **Next** and **Previous** button behavior in the workflow is to have a pool variable called `nextStep` and every time the **Next** or **Previous** button is clicked, we can set the `nextStep` variable to the name of the step, and in the transitions from one step to another we can check for the value of `nextStep`.

1. In the form, first make a backward transition from all the steps that are the endpoints of the forward transition. The final pool should look like this:

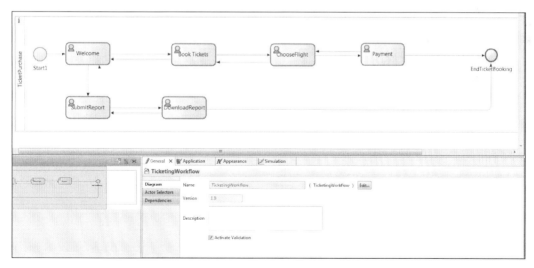

Figure 3.11: Workflow after adding backward transitions

2. Now, open the first form of the workflow, **Welcome**, and click on the **BookTickets** button.

3. In the **Actions** tab, add an action that sets the next step to the variable `nextStep`. The way to do this is by inputting `BookTickets` in the Groovy script in the expressions field and saving it to the variable `nextStep`.

4. Similarly, in the **SubmitReport** button, type `SubmitReport` in the Groovy script, and save it to `nextStep`. Looking at the workflow, there are two forward transitions from the **Welcome** step. Hence, the engine doesn't know which one to go to. For this reason, we have to put conditions on the transitions so that only one of them can be true at a time.

5. Click on the transition pointing towards **SubmitReport** and in the condition window enter `nextStep=="SubmitReport"` (those are two equal to signs).

6. Similarly, in the transition towards **BookTickets**, enter the condition as `'nextStep=="BookTickets"'`. We now see that when the user clicks on the button, it is set to `nextStep` and only the transition for which `nextStep` is equal to that button click is true. Hence, our purpose is achieved.

We shall adopt a similar strategy for the other **Next** and **Previous** buttons as well.

1. Open the **BookTickets** web form and select the **Submit** button. In the expression of a new action on the button, we enter `ChooseFlight` and save it to the `nextStep` variable.

2. Similarly, in the **Back** button, we enter `Welcome`. Now, in the transition leading from **BookTickets** to **ChooseFlight**, we enter `nextStep=="ChooseFlight"` and in the transition from **BookTickets** to **Welcome**, we enter `nextStep=="Welcome"`.

3. We can do the same thing for the remaining steps. After this, we have almost completed our design of the workflow. It is now time to run it. Before that, click on the pool and in the **Application** tab select **Look'n'feel**.

4. Click on **Apply a Look'n'feel** and select **White**. It is now time to run the application.

5. Click on **Run** and the welcome screen pops up. Click on the **Submit Report** button and you will be navigated to the **Submit Report** web page.

Figure 3.12: Submit Report web page

6. Let us attach a document and write some comments. Click on **Submit**. We get a confirmation box stating that the information has been submitted.

7. Go back to the inbox page and click on **Logout**. Now, log in as `tim` and we see that the item is waiting in his inbox as it has been submitted to him. Click on the red rectangle on the right-hand side of the row item and the form opens up in a new window.

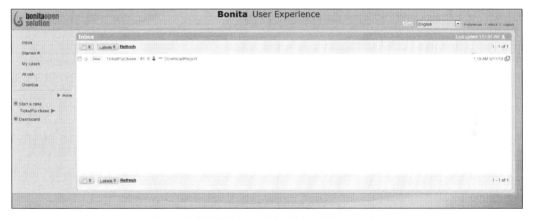

Figure 3.13: The inbox of the flightadmin user tim

We have made the workflow in this chapter.

Summary

We have learned how to create web forms in this chapter. We have used the different elements present in the palette to make web forms that suit our purpose. We have learned how to create pool and step variables and also how the action button works. In addition, we learned how to give conditions to transitions. In the following chapter, we will learn how to use connectors.

4
Conditions, Contingencies, and Transitions

In the previous chapter, we created web forms for the steps of the **Ticketing** workflow. We laid out the basic framework of the forms and populated some of the data in it. Here, we will look at the various conditions on the various form elements, the contingencies that might exist among the form elements, and also the transitions from one step to another. At the end of this chapter, we will know how to enhance our existing workflow with these elements and conditions.

Conditional appearance of fields

We did explore the option of the conditional appearance of fields in the last chapter while defining the passenger information in the Payment step. For most of the widgets, there is an option to insert the widget in the form only if a particular condition is satisfied. If not, the widget isn't inserted in the form at all. This is different from inserting the widget and hiding it using JavaScript or some other script. Here, the widget isn't inserted into the form at all. Click on the **Options** tab of any widget and tick the check box for **Insert widget if** and in the expression box we can either enter a Boolean variable or write a Groovy script that returns true or false. As expected, the widget is inserted only if the expression evaluates to true. Note that we cannot use any field value of other widgets present on the form in the Groovy script. We have to use pool variables or step variables or some other Groovy condition. Let us write a Groovy expression that returns a Boolean value.

For evaluating a condition, we make use of logical operators in Groovy. We evaluate three conditions separated by logical AND and OR conditions. The logical AND is written as && in Groovy/Java and logical OR is written as ||. In the first expression, we check if a String equals a particular value. This always returns true or false. Next, we parse a String value as an Integer value and check if it is greater than a particular value. In the third expression, we compare a Long variable with a value.

```
arrival.equals("New York") && (Integer.parseInt(passengerNumber) >
   5 || price < 2000
```

Figure 4.1: Evaluating a Groovy expression for conditional appearance of fields

Here, we evaluate strings and integers as an example. Depending on the need, we can write any expression here and return true or false. The Groovy editor here can be used for evaluating conditions, but it is in fact more powerful and can be used for setting variables, evaluating complex conditions, and so on. You can read more about Groovy at http://groovy.codehaus.org/Documentation.

Contingency

The contingency feature is available only in the Subscription Pack version of Bonita Studio, which is essentially a paid version. There are ways to manage the contingencies with JavaScript, but it is often tedious. Bonita provides this as an additional feature in the Subscription Pack. Hence, if you have bought the Subscription Pack, you are all ready to use these contingencies.

A contingency can be defined on a particular widget. This contingency can be about the visibility of the widget and also about the values that are made available in the data section of the widget. Let us get down to an example to test the contingency.

1. Open the **BookTickets** web form and click on the **Return date** widget. In the **Contingency** tab of this widget, we can specify the behavior of this widget based on certain contingencies. What we would like to do is that, if the user clicks on **One way trip**, the **Return date** widget should not be shown, but if he/she clicks on **Return trip**, he/she should be shown the return widget to pick the return date. This functionality can be easily achieved by the contingency feature.
2. Click on the **Contingency** tab and we can see that there is a list of widgets on which the data field of this particular widget is contingent. Right now, the list is empty. Let us add the **TripOptions** widget as a contingency.
3. Click on **Add...** and select **TripOptions**. We now see that the **Return date** widget is contingent on the trip options.
4. Now, on the right-hand side pane, we have three options. The first one is the condition for this particular widget to be shown on form load. Now, the default option for the trip is a **One way trip**. Hence, this **Return date** widget should not be shown when the page loads. Hence, we make this value false.
5. Change `true` to `false` in the expression field. In the next field, we have an option to show this widget when a contingent field has changed. Now, for the **Return date** widget, we have added **TripOptions** as a contingent field. Hence, here we define the condition for the **Return date** widget to be shown or not.
6. Click on **Edit expression...** to open the **Groovy editor**.

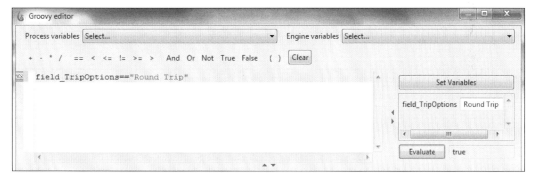

Figure 4.2: Groovy expression to define contingency

Conditions, Contingencies, and Transitions

In the **Groovy editor**, we can use the available field variables of the contingent widgets. The field variables are the variables that are currently filled or selected by the user when the form is opened. All the field variables in Bonita are named `field_` followed by the name of the widget. To see all the field variables you can use in your current Groovy script, you can check them in the **Process variables** drop-down list at the top of the **Groovy editor**, or just type `field_` and press *Ctrl* + Space bar (the way you might do in Eclipse) and Groovy lists down all the field variables that you can use. For this groovy expression, we need to insert the widget only if the radio button for **Round Trip** is chosen. We do this by checking if the field value of the **TripOptions** widget is set to **Round Trip**. In Groovy, enter the following expression:

```
field_TripOptions=="Round Trip"
```

The third field is the update value field. For this widget, we don't have to update any value as it is a date picker. But there may be times when the available values of any field might change due to certain conditions. Let us look at an example of this, too.

1. Click on the **Passengers** drop-down widget.
2. Add **TripOptions** as a data field on which **Passengers** is contingent. Leave the **Show immediately** field and **Show if a contingent field has changed** to **True**.
3. Now the value for this widget can be made to change every time the contingent field has changed. In the available values after the update field, let us make an array list of Strings, where we give the passenger options. Enter the following code in the groovy expression:

    ```
    List passengerContingency = new ArrayList<String>();
    if(field_TripOptions=="Round Trip") {
      passengerContingency.add("One");
      passengerContingency.add("Two");
      passengerContingency.add("Three");
    } else {
      passengerContingency.add("1");
      passengerContingency.add("2");
      passengerContingency.add("3");
    }
    return passengerContingency;
    ```

4. In the previous code, we create a new array list of Strings. Depending on whether the selected field of **TripOptions** is **Round Trip** or **One way trip**, we add values to this list. At the end, we return this list.

5. In the next field, **Selected value after update**, enter the following Groovy code:
   ```
   if(field_TripOptions=="Round Trip") {
     return "Two";
   } else {
     return "1";
   }
   ```

6. Here, depending on whether the selected **TripOptions** field is **One Way trip** or **Round Trip**, we return the initial value of the drop-down box.

If the radio button is selected as **One way trip**, the default **passengerOptions** list of options is available in the drop-down options, with the default value as **1**. But if **Round Trip** is selected as the value of the **Trip Options** widget, then we make a new list of Strings, and **2** is selected as the default option. We can see how this works by running the application and looking at the form.

Similarly, we can add the contingencies to the widgets we want. We can also make a widget contingent on many fields. All these options can be explored according to the requirements.

The JavaScript alternative to the contingency feature

If you are using the Community Edition of Bonitasoft, you can't use contingencies. In that case, there are certain alternatives we can look at. We can use any scripting language, such as JavaScript or JQuery, to achieve what contingencies do. **HTML widget** is available in the palette section of the form design. In this widget, it is possible to write the JavaScript functions and code. Let us use JavaScript in **HTML widget** to conditionally display the **Return Trip** date in the **BookTickets** step.

In the **BookTickets** web form, let us drag a new **HTML widget** from the palette to the bottom of the form.

> **HTML widget** should be placed beneath all the other widgets for it to access the other widgets. If the other widgets are beneath **HTML widget**, then **HTML widget** will not be able to access the data or any attributes of these widgets.

Whenever we add a new widget in web forms, we give it a name. This name is used by Bonita to assign the same ID to the HTML element it generates while creating the HTML page with all the elements of the Web form. This is really useful while writing JavaScript and for automated Web Browser testing using tools such as Selenium. You can find more information at http://www.seleniumhq.org/.

In the **Data** section of **HTML widget**, enter the following JavaScript code:

```
<script>
function changeDateVisibility()
{
  if(document.getElementById('TripOptions').getElementsByTagName
    ('input')[0].checked==true)
  document.getElementById('Return').style.visibility='hidden';
  else
  document.getElementById('Return').style.visibility='visible';
}
document.getElementById('Return').style.visibility='hidden';
</script>
```

We define a JavaScript function called `changeDateVisiblity`. This function checks the condition for the **TripOptions** radio button selected, **One way trip** or **Round Trip**. The `getElementsByTagName('input')[0]` command refers to the **One way trip** option. If it is checked, then we should hide the return date picker. Else, we should make it visible. After the function, we write a JavaScript function to hide the return date picker. This is done because, when the form loads for the first time, the default option is one way and hence the return date picker should not be shown at the beginning. When the user makes any change in the **TripOptions** widget, the JavaScript code should be triggered. For this, go to the **TripOptions** widget and select the **Options** tab. Here, in the **Html Attributes**, enter the following code:

```
onchange='changeDateVisibility()'
```

This **Html Attribute** defines that the function `changeDateVisiblity` is called on change of any selection in this widget.

Similarly, we can use JavaScript to update the values of fields without making use of contingencies.

Defining conditions on transitions

In the last chapter, we have defined various transitions for the steps. We can also define conditions on these transitions such that one particular transition holds true in some situation. Thus, there can be many transitions from one step to the others, but depending on which transition is true we can proceed to the next step.

For defining the condition on the transitions, we can use the **Edit expression...** option to define a groovy script which returns a `true` or `false` Boolean value depending on the conditions. If the value returned is `true`, the transition becomes active. We have already seen how to return a Boolean value from a groovy expression.

Gates

Often, we require gates in our process diagrams when we have complex transitions between steps. Gates help to define a variety of transitions, loops, and circuits. Let us have a look at the three different types of gates available in Bonita Studio:

1. **XOR gate**: An XOR or exclusive gateway is most commonly used during merging conditions when any of the two or more steps need to be completed for the workflow to move ahead. When there are multiple inputs to an XOR gateway, the process will move to the output of the XOR gateway when any one of the input conditions becomes true. If there are multiple outputs for an XOR gateway, all the transitions will be randomly evaluated one by one and the first true condition will be evaluated and the process will move forward without evaluating the other transitions.

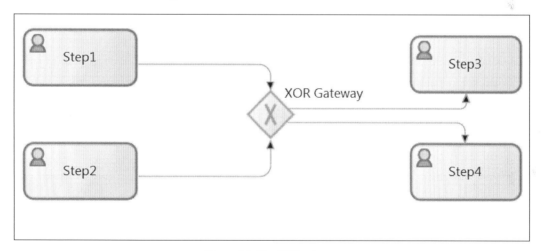

Figure 4.3: The XOR gateway

2. **AND gate**: An AND gate is used in cases when certain activities need to be carried out in parallel. The AND gate is both convergent and divergent. In the case of convergent inputs, all inputs must arrive at the gate before the flow passes through the gateway. In the case of divergent outputs, all the outputs will be enabled in parallel when the flow passes through the AND gate.

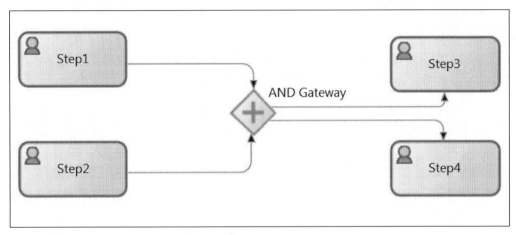

Figure 4.4: The AND gateway

In the preceding figure, the AND gateway will not be enabled till both **Step1** and **Step2** are completed. When they are completed, **Step3** and **Step4** will be triggered and they move in parallel.

3. **Inclusive gateway**: The inputs to the Inclusive gateway are treated as an XOR gate and the outputs are treated as an AND gate.

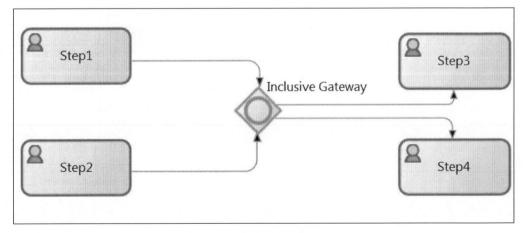

Figure 4.5: The Inclusive gateway

In the previous figure, if either **Step1** or **Step2** completes first, the process flow moves to the Inclusive gateway and then **Step3** and **Step4** are triggered simultaneously in parallel.

Passing the message

Message events are used to pass the data from one pool to the other. The pool variables that we declare inside a pool may be required in some other pool. For this, we use the message passing event, where we basically send a message from one pool to the other. A single message is sent from a pool and the target can receive a single message. This can be useful in synchronizing the two processes.

As data cannot be passed from one pool to another, we achieve this feature using a message passing activity. The data between the throw message and the catch message needs to be mapped so as that it is made available at the target pool.

There are basically two types of message events in Bonita. One is an intermediary throw and catch message which can send data across pools. Another type is the message passing event, that is either a start or an end message. An end message ends the process and sends a message containing the data. A start message catches a message with the data and starts the process.

Let us create an example of a message passing event.

1. In our **TicketingWorkflow** process, let us add another pool called `Payment` beneath the **TicketPurchase** pool. After the payment details in the **TicketPurchase** pool, let us send a message containing the payment details to the **Payment** pool via a message passing event.

2. Drag an end message event from the palette and place it next to the **Payment** step in the **TicketPurchase** pool. Change the transition from the **Payment** step to point to this new end message step. We name this step `PaymentMessage`.

3. Now, we need to define a new message for this step, which will contain the data that we need to pass to the next pool.

4. In the **Payment** pool, drag a new start message. Rename this as `PaymentReceiver`. We will now create the message to be passed from one pool to another.

5. Click on **Add...** in the **Messages** tab of the step to define a new message. We can call this message `PaymentMessage`. In the target pool, select **Payment** and in the target task, select **PaymentReceiver**. The default expiry of the message is set to `1 year`. We can change it according to the requirements, but for most cases we can let it remain `1 year`.

6. On the next page, we add the data that we have to send to the other pool. Note that we would have to create new variables for this purpose, whose default values can be the variables we would like to send the data across. In this message, let us send the payment related information to the other pool.

7. Click on **Add...** and define a new text variable called `messageCardHolder`, with the default value as `cardholder`, which we can select from the drop-down option.

8. Similarly, we should define other variables, all named `messageX`, where `X` is the original name of the variable we want to pass to the new pool. Let us pass `cardNumber`, `cvv`, `month`, and `year` variables to the **Payment** pool. Once we define that, click on **OK**.

9. We should now see a dotted transition from the end message step to the start message step in the **Payment** pool. We have completed one part of the message passing event, namely, sending variables from one pool to the next.

10. Now, we have to receive the message in the other pool and set the variables accordingly.

Chapter 4

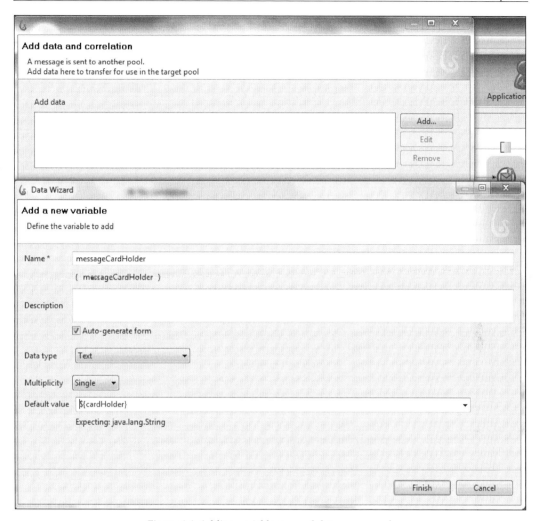

Figure 4.6: Adding variables to send data across pools

11. For us to capture the information required in the **Payment** pool, we first need to create the pool variables for saving the data that is received. Hence, create the text variables for **cardHolder**, **cardNumber**, **cvv**, **month**, and **year** in the **Payment** pool.

12. Next, click on the **Start Message** step. Here, we see that in the **General** tab, the **Catch Event** option is set to **PaymentMessage**. This **Start Message** step catches the data from the other pool, but it doesn't set it to the pool variables, because the mapping hasn't been defined yet.

Conditions, Contingencies, and Transitions

We achieve this by the use of connectors. Although we will delve into the different kinds of connectors in the next chapter, let us introduce one connector here that is essential for catching the data from the other pool and setting the value of the variables in the new pool.

13. On the **Start Message** step, click on the **Connectors** tab and select **Add...**. We get a plethora of connector options. Here, we will make use of a **Bonita** connector.
14. Expand the **Bonita** connector and select the connector **Set Variables -- Set process or step variables**. This connector is used to set a number of Bonita variables in one single connector. Let us name this variable `setPoolVariables`.
15. After clicking on **Next**, we are greeted with a table, where we can set a variable name and its value. The variable name should be the target pool variable and the variable value should be the data that came along with the message.
16. Click on **Add a row** to start mapping the variables. Map all the variables that were sent in the message. After doing so, you should be left with the following:

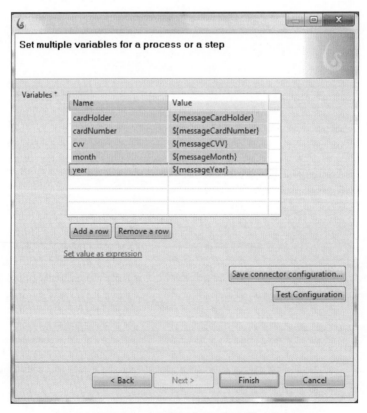

Figure 4.7: Mapping variables in Set Variables connector

[62]

17. After clicking on **Finish**, we are done with the steps required for passing the data from one pool to the other using the message passing event.

This event is mostly used to send data from one pool to the other, although it can be used for some other purposes too.

The call activity

A call activity step in Bonita is like a function call in programming languages. Here a pool is called by a call activity, unlike a function. After the called pool completes, the control is passed back to the calling step. A mapping is defined from the parent pool to the subpool and a reverse mapping is also possible.

Let us illustrate the call activity in our **TicketingWorkflow**. One thing we notice is that we can separate out the report submission tasks into a separate pool. This is due to the fact that this task doesn't use the pool variables that we use for booking a ticket, nor are the variables used in this task useful in booking a ticket. Hence, it makes sense to separate out this activity.

1. Make a new pool called Report and add all the variables necessary for the report submission in this new pool, namely, report, reportSubmitter, and comments. Delete the two variables, except reportSubmitter, from the **TicketPurchase** pool.

2. Next, copy the two steps from the **TicketPurchase** pool to the new **Report** pool. This can be done by selecting these two steps and either navigating to **Edit | Copy**, or by pressing *Ctrl + C*. Paste these two steps in the new pool. Bonita renames these two steps as a copy of the original names. We can change the name back to the original name and delete the steps from the **TicketPurchase** workflow.

3. Now, drag a call activity from the palette and place it beneath the **Welcome** step. Name this step `InitiateReport`. In the **General** tab of this step we have the option to select the subprocess. Select **Report** from the drop-down options. The process figure will now look like the following screenshot:

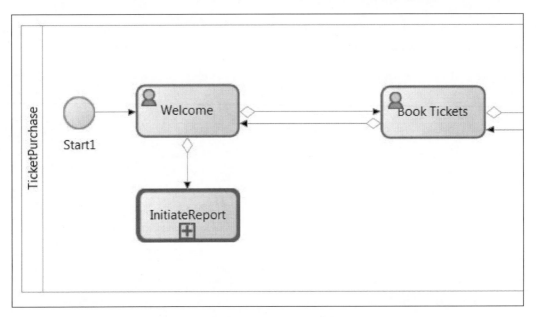

Figure 4.8: The InitiateReport call activity

4. First, before we map certain variables, we need to make sure that the initiator is saved to the `reportSubmitter` variable when we click on the **SubmitReport** button at the **Welcome** step.

5. Open the **Welcome** web form, select the **SubmitReport** button and go to the **Actions** tab. Add an action and in the expression field write the following code in the Groovy editor:

```
return loggedUser;
```

6. Save it to the variable called `reportSubmitter`. Now, we have to map this variable to the **Report** pool.

7. Click on the **InitiateReport** task and go to the **Mapping** tab. Here, we define the mapping from the source process to the subprocess. Let us add the mapping for the `reportSubmitter`.

8. Click on the add button and in the **Source data** field select **reportSubmitter** from the drop-down options. These options are the pool variables that are available. This variable is assigned to some variable which we have to define.

9. In the **Subprocess data** field, select **reportSubmitter**. Note that this **reportSubmitter** variable is the pool variable for the **Report** pool. We could have alternatively auto-mapped the source process variables and the subprocess variables. This can be done if both the source variable and the target variable have the same name or the subprocess data is prefixed with sub_. This is useful in cases where we have to map a lot of variables.

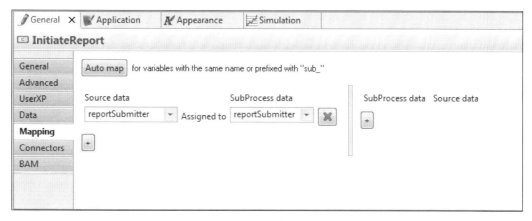

Figure 4.9: Mapping for a call activity

When the control comes to the **InitiateReport** step, it spawns the **Report** pool. Now, we have to add starting and end signals to the **Report** pool. After adding the starting and end events, click on the **SubmitReport** web form and in the **SubmitReportMessage**, change `loggedUser` in the data to `reportSubmitter`. When the **Report** pool is over, the control is passed back to the **InitiateReport** step in the **TicketPurchase** pool. Here, we can add additional steps, but for now, let us end the flow. Hence, define a transition from **InitiateReport** to the end event.

Multiinstantiation

Multi instantiation is used in the case when we want the same step to be repeated a number of times. There are some options that we can configure when it comes to multi instantiation. Let us look at these options via an example. Right now, the initiator can only submit one report at a time. Let us give him/her the option to choose the number of reports he/she should submit and thereafter multi instantiate the whole **Report** pool those many number of times. For this, let us create a new form in between the **Welcome** and the **InitiateReport** step. Let us call this step `ReportNumber`. Create a web form for this step, with a radio button widget called `ReportNumberOptions`. Change its label to `Select the number of reports to be submitted:`.

Conditions, Contingencies, and Transitions

We also need to create the data for the radio button options. Hence, for this reason, create a step variable called `reportNumberOptions`, with the data type **Passengers**. Note that we had already created the list of options for **Passengers** in the previous chapter, with the values as 1, 2, and 3. Also, create a pool integer variable called `count`, where we shall store the report number value selected by the user. In the **ReportNumberOptions** widget, select the data type as **reportNumberOptions**, and in the expression value enter the following groovy command:

```
return Long.parseLong(field_ReportNumberOptions);
```

When the user selects a particular report number, it is stored as a string. We need to convert this into the Long variable so that we can perform mathematical operations on it. For this purpose, we use the standard way of converting a string to a Long data type. In the **save to** field, enter `count`. Change the label of **Submit1** to `Submit`. Make sure that there is a transition from the **Welcome** step to the **ReportNumber** step and from this step to the **InitiateReport** step. We now plan to multi instantiate the whole **Report** pool. For this, all we need to do is to multi instantiate the **InitiateReport** call activity.

Figure 4.10: Instantiator for a multi-instantiated step

1. Click on **InitiateReport** and navigate to the **Advanced** tab of the step. Here, we find the radio button options of **None**, **is Multi-Instantiated**, and **is Looped**. By default it's always **None**, but we have to select **is Multi-Instantiated**. The moment we select that, two fields, **Instantiator** and **Join Checker**, appear on the screen.

   The **Instantiator** field is where we define the premise for instantiation—the number of times the particular step is multi-instantiated. The **Join Checker** is a field where we define the number of instances after which the control passes to the next step. First, let us select the **Instantiator** option.

2. Click on **Browse...** and from the available options, select **Number of instances -- Specify number of instances** as the instantiator. We can name this `ReportNumberInstantiator`.

3. After clicking on **Next**, we get an option to choose the number of instances. Select **count** from the drop-down options.

4. Click on **Finish** to be done with the instantiator.

5. We move on to the **Join Checker** option. Browse through the options and select percentage of completed instances. In the next page, we specify the percentage to be completed until we move on to the next step. The next step in this case is the end of the workflow, as the **Report** pool is a call activity and not a next step. Hence, we want all instances of the **Report** pool to be completed before the workflow ends.

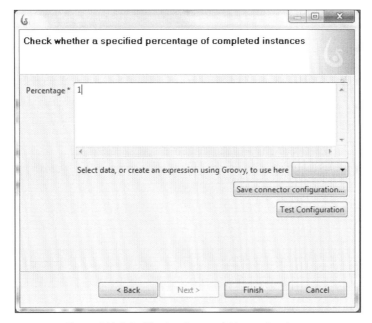

Figure 4.11: Join Checker for a multi-instantiated step

Conditions, Contingencies, and Transitions

We have now defined the steps to multi-instantiate the **Report** pool. We will also add some ability to pass different values of the same variable to different instantiations.

We have defined the number of reports, but we don't have any way to distinguish one report from the other. For this, we will define a `reportNumber` variable that we will pass to the **Report** pool. This integer will contain the particular report number. Create a new pool integer variable, called `reportNumber`, with the default value as 0. Create the integer variable `reportNumber` in the **Report** pool too. We would also need to add this to the mapping of the **InitiateReport** step. Once we do that, the value of the variable `reportNumber` is copied from the calling pool to the target pool. Thus, we can get to know the particular report number in the **Report** pool.

Next, we need to display this `reportNumber` in the **Report** pool. We shall do that in the **SubmitReport** web form. In this form, change the label by entering the following groovy script:

```
"Report Number " + String.valueOf(reportNumber) + " :"
```

Now, we need to increment the value of `reportNumber` for each time the multi instantiation works. We can do this by defining a connector at the start of the **InitiateReport** step, where we increment the value of `reportNumber`. Note that the default value of `reportNumber` is 0. When we define a start connector at the starting of the multi instantiation step, this start connector is run for each of the instantiations. Hence, if we keep incrementing the value of `reportNumber` for every instantiation, different values for `reportNumber` get passed on to the **Report** pool. Thus, we can differentiate between various instantiations.

Even though we will define connectors in the next chapter, here we will define a connector that runs a groovy script. Click on the **InitiateReport** step, and navigate to the **Connectors** tab. Here, click on **Add...** and from the various connector options, select groovy from the **Scripting** option. Let's call this connector `IncrementReportNumber`.

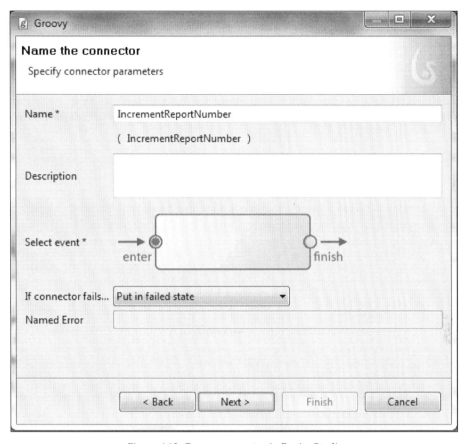

Figure 4.12: Groovy connector in Bonita Studio

In the **Select event** option, choose **enter**. This means that this connector will be executed when the control enters this step. Similarly, we can also define the course of action when the connector fails. We can put the workflow in a failed state, ignore, or throw an error. In the following screenshot, we have to define a script by which we can choose **Edit expression...** to bring up the Groovy expression box. Enter the following line in the script:

```
reportNumber += 1;
```

Click on **Finish** and we are done with the connector. This connector runs every time the **Report** pool is instantiated. Hence, we have a way to distinguish the different instances of the **Report** pool.

Once we run the workflow, we will be able to check the difference the multi instantiation and call activity have made. Go to the **TicketPurchase** pool and select **Run**. Click on the **Submit Report** button and select **3** as the number of reports to be submitted. After you click on **Submit**, you will be taken to the **SubmitReport** form. Here, you will see that the report to be submitted is report number three. This is because the report number three is the latest to be spawned by the multi instantiation. Go back to the inbox without filling this form. You will notice that the inbox has changed and now shows three tasks to be done.

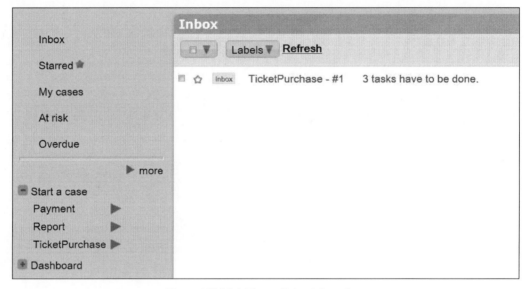

Figure 4.13: Multi Instantiation inbox view

This is a collapsed list. If you click on this, a new view will open with the three tasks listed. We can click on these tasks and complete them.

Summary

This section introduced the concepts of conditions, transitions, and contingencies. We learned how to make use of JavaScript if contingencies aren't present. We also gained insight about the call activity and the multi instantiation of a process in Bonita. In addition, we found out the way to pass data from one pool to another using a message passing event.

In the next chapter, we will discuss the various kinds of connectors in Bonita and how to use them.

5
Adding Connectors

We had a look at how to define conditions, transitions, and contingencies in the previous chapter. These features allowed us to modify the existing steps and web forms according to our needs. Here we will introduce the connectors available in Bonita. Connectors, as the name suggests, are used to get data in and out of Bonita via various means. We also have the ability to send e-mails, make calendar appointments, and so on, via connectors. Bonita Studio has a lot of connectors pre-defined and we only have to fill in the various parameters to make them work.

Connectors are a powerful functionality provided by Bonita that makes it easy to integrate with other third-party applications. This is a nifty and useful feature that makes Bonita Open Solution an ideal platform for integrating different data at a single place.

Types of connectors in Bonita

Click on any step, navigate to the **Connectors** tab and click on **Add...**. We are greeted with a huge list of connectors. The connectors bundled under the **Bonita** category are related to the workflow itself. We can modify various steps and variables of the workflow using these connectors. The database connectors are already configured for most of the famous databases in use and they only need connection parameters to connect to the databases. We can execute SQL queries and modify the result set using these database connectors. We also have **Drools** connectors that make use of the Drools engine to execute custom-defined rules. In addition, we have some connectors for calendar and events, and integration with LDAP, SAP, Salesforce, and other popular web services. There's also a connector for executing a Java class and another for sending an e-mail through the workflow. We have a couple of connectors for scripting purposes, too.

Adding Connectors

We will look at some of these connectors in detail, and provide certain examples of how we can use them in the workflow we created.

Let us have a look at the various connectors available in Bonita:

- **Alfresco**
- **Bonita**
- **CMIS**
- **Database**
- **Drools**
- **Exchange**
- **Google**
- **Jasper**
- **Java**
- **LDAP**
- **Messaging**
- **SAP**
- **Salesforce**
- **Scripting**
- **Sharepoint**
- **Sheetster**
- **Social**
- **SugarCRM**
- **Talend**
- **Web Services**
- **XWiki**
- **eXo**

As we can see, Bonita has the ability to integrate data from all the major third-party tools. The logic can be developed in Bonita and the data can be fetched through the connectors. Hence, we can develop a platform for integrating different data together.

Before we start exploring the connectors, let us define the key parameters to be defined in a connector. Every connector is identified by a unique name. This name should be unique across all the pools in the workflow. Next, we define the **Select Event** parameter. This selection states at which part of the step the connector will run. For human tasks, we have options of **enter**, **start**, **suspend**, **resume**, and **finish**. If the connector is meant to be run at enter, then it is initiated right when the workflow moves to this step. Start is when the connector will be run at the start of the step. In the User XP, we can suspend and resume a step. When the step is suspended, the connector that is defined at suspension will be invoked. Similarly, if the step is resumed, then the connector invoked at resume will work. Finally, the finish connector is invoked after the particular form of a step has been submitted. Note that for a service step, we have only two options for the **Select event** parameter: **start** and **finish**. This is because a service step cannot be suspended or resumed.

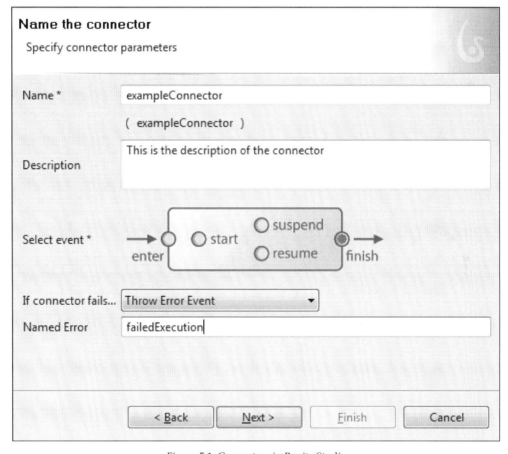

Figure 5.1: Connectors in Bonita Studio

Next we have the option to define the course of action if the connector fails. The first option is to put the workflow in failed state. There is no way to recover from a failed state workflow. A new instance has to be created for moving ahead. When the step fails, the reason for failure can be found in the logs. This might be a generic error as the logging is done by Bonita and may not reflect which part of the connector failed. The second option is to ignore the error and continue the process. In this case, even if there is an error, the workflow continues. The connector may fail and certain data may not be available for the next step. The last option is to throw a named error event. We can define the named error in the box for the field **Named Error** as shown in the previous screenshot. The next step is generally where we write the most important part of the connector.

Let us have a look at these connectors one by one and look at examples of them:

Bonita connectors

Bonita connectors are used to set variables or some other parameters inside Bonita. They can also be used to start a process or execute a step. These connectors equip the user to connect with different parameters of the Bonita workflow. The other kind of connectors are used to integrate with some other third-party tools.

Most of the **Bonita** connectors are related to the documents and comments at a particular step. Although these may be useful in some cases, in a majority of the cases we will not find much use for them. The most useful ones are getting the users a step, executing a step, starting a new process, and setting variables.

Click on any step on which you want to define the connector and click on **Add....** Here, we will check the start an instance connector of Bonita. Give a name to this connector and click on **Next**. Here we have to fill in the name of the process that we want to invoke. We also have an option to specify different versions of the process. If we leave this blank, it will pick up the latest version. Next, we can specify the process variables that need to be copied from one pool to the other.

Chapter 5

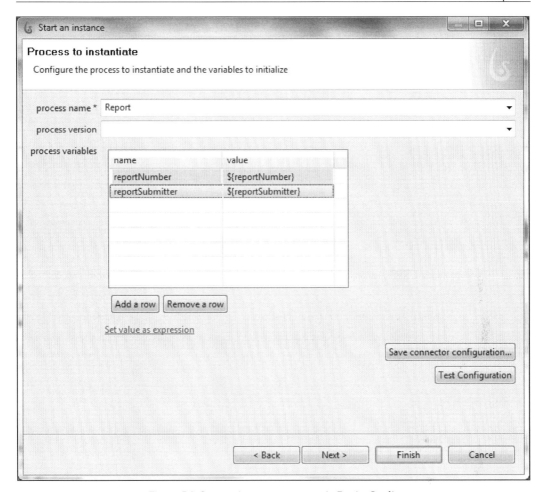

Figure 5.2: Start an instance connector in Bonita Studio

In the previous example, the process variables that we specify will be copied over to the target pool. We have to make sure that the target pool has the process variables mentioned in this connector.

Make sure that you mention the name of the variable in the first column without the curly braces. If you select the names from the drop-down menu, make sure you remove the $ and the { } for filling in the name.

The value field can be filled by the actual process variable.

We can also use the set variable connector to set a value to a variable, either a process variable or a step variable. Here, we have two parameters: one is the variable whose value we have to set and the other parameter is the actual value of the variable. Note that this value may be a Groovy expression, too. Hence, it is similar to writing a Groovy script to assign a value to a variable.

Another type of connector is the one to start or finish a step. In this connector, all we have to do is mention the name of the step we want to start or stop. Similarly, there is another connector to execute a step. Executing will run all the start and end connectors of a particular step and then finish it. These connectors might be useful in the cases where some step may be waiting for another step, and at the end of the current step we might execute that step or mark it finished.

We also have connectors to get the users from the workflow. There are connectors to find out the initiator of a process and the step submitter. Another useful connector is to get a user based on the username. This returns the User class that Bonita uses to implement the functionality of a user in the workflow. Select the connector to get a user from a username. Enter the username and click on **Next**. Here, we get the output of the connector and we can decide to save the output in a particular pool or step variable.

Chapter 5

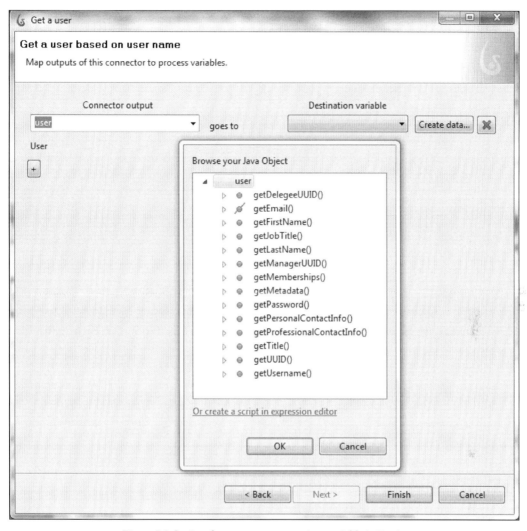

Figure 5.3: Saving the connector output in a variable in Bonita

The `user` class has methods to retrieve data, such as the e-mail, first name, last name, metadata, and password from the user.

Adding Connectors

The e-mail connector

We have a connector in the messaging group to send an e-mail. Now, we might use this connector for a variety of purposes: to send information about the workflow to an external e-mail, to send a notification to the person performing the task that he/she has some pending items in his/her inbox, and so on. We have to configure the e-mail connector on various parameters.

In our **TicketingWorkflow**, let us send an e-mail to the person in whose name the tickets are booked. He/she enters his/her e-mail address in the **Payment** step of the workflow. Hence, let us send an e-mail at the end of the **Payment** step to the person at his/her e-mail address with which the tickets have been booked. For this, let us configure the e-mail connector:

1. Click on the **Payment** step of the workflow.
2. Click on the **Connectors** tab to add a connector. Select the connector as a medium to send an e-mail. Then name the connector as `SendEmail` and make sure that this connector is at the finish event of the step.
3. In the next step, we are required to enter the configuration details of the SMTP server we will use for sending the e-mail. By default, it is set to the Gmail configuration with the host as `smtp.gmail.com` and the port as `465`. Let us stick to the default option and send an e-mail from a Gmail hosted server.
4. Leave the **Security** option as it is, but enter your credentials in the **Authentication** section. Here, you should enter your full e-mail address, not just your username. You can also use your own domain e-mail address if it is hosted on a Gmail server.
5. Next, we define the parameters of the e-mail notification that has to be sent. After entering the **From** address as the ticketing admin address or some similar address, enter the **To** address as the variable in which we have saved the e-mail address: `email`.
6. In the title field, we have to specify the subject of the e-mail. We have already seen that we can use Java inside the Groovy editor. Here, we will have a look at a simple Java code that is executed inside the editor. Enter the following code in the Groovy editor:

    ```
    import java.text.SimpleDateFormat;
    return "Flight ticket from " + from + " to " + to + " on "
      + new SimpleDateFormat("MM-dd-yyyy").format(departOn);
    ```

7. The overview of the flight details is mentioned in the subject of the e-mail. We know that the `departOn` variable is a Date object. For printing the date, we have to convert it into a String by using the `SimpleDateFormat` class.

8. Next, we have to write the actual e-mail that we will send to the customer. Below the **Title** field, make sure that the e-mail body is in **HTML** and not plain text. We can insert Groovy scripts in between the text, which will be substituted with the actual variable value when the e-mail is sent. Write the following in the body of the e-mail:

   `Hi ${passenger1},`

   `Your ${from} to ${to} flight is confirmed. The flight details are given below:`

Date	Departure	Arrival	Duration	Price
`${import java.text.SimpleDateFormat; return new SimpleDateFormat("MM-dd-yyyy").format(departOn);`	`${departure}`	`${arrival}`	`${duration}`	`${price}`

   `Travelers:`

   `${passenger1}`

   `${passenger2}`

   `${passenger3}`

   `Payment Details:`

   `Card Holder - ${cardHolder}`

   `Card Number - ${cardNumber}`

Adding Connectors

```
Thank you for booking with TicketingWorkflow!
```

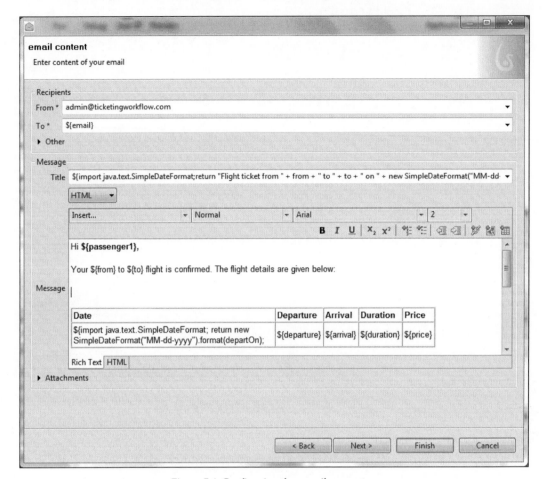

Figure 5.4: Configuring the e-mail connector

9. Clicking on **Next** will get you to the advanced options. Generally it's not really required to configure these options, and we can make do with the default settings.

The Drools connector

Another set of connectors that might be used is the **Drools** connector. Here we will see how we make use of a .drl file to check the business rule that has to be applied. In the following section, let us look at a simple example of using **Drools**. However, for more knowledge about **Drools** and its terminology, please visit http://www.jboss.org/drools/documentation.

[80]

A DRL file is a DocObject Resource Locator file, that contains rules for implementing some logic. In a nutshell, a drools file contains a variety of rules, which are similar to a lot of `if-else` statements.

A sample drools file may contain rules like the following one:

```
package com.company.license;
import com.company.entities.Applicant;
rule "Is of valid age"
when
    $a : Applicant( age < 18 )
then
    $a.setValid( false );
end
```

In a drools file, we have a set of rules in a `when` and `then` format, followed by the key word `end`. In the previous example, we have a rule called "Is of valid age", where we check if the variable age in the object `Applicant` is more than 18. If so, we invoke the `setValid` function of the object `Applicant` and set it to `true`. Note that `$a` is used to denote the object `Applicant`, and in the `then` clause we invoke the `setValid` method of `$a`.

This is just one example of how a rule works. There may be complex rules with a variety of objects. For us to make use of the drools file, we make use of the drools engine. We supply a list of objects to the drools engine and this engine checks this list against the DRL file, modifies the list if it finds any relevant rule, and returns the list.

Let us now see how the **Drools** connector works in Bonita. Add a connector in Bonita. In the **Drools** group, select the **StatelessKnowledgeSession** (read more about it at `http://docs.jboss.org/drools/release/5.2.0.M2/drools-expert-docs/html/ch02.html`). This connector is used to execute a list of facts in the stateless knowledge session mode using a `.drl` file. In the parameters that we have to specify, the first one is the DRL file path. Here, we have to give the complete file path of the location of the drools file. Let us say that we have a drools file called `ValidAge.drl` on your desktop, containing the previous given code. Then the file path of the file would be `C:\\Users\\rohit.bhat\\Desktop\\ValidAge.drl`.

The path would change according to your system. Next, there is an option to specify the list of facts. This would be a list of elements that we supply to the **Drools** connector. Now, let us see which elements we need to include in this array. If we take the drools file as it is, it makes use of only one object, that is, `Applicant`. So, the drools engine expects the list of facts to contain only one object. But if the DRL file contains rules compassing multiple objects, we send these objects as an array.

Adding Connectors

We need to use the `Applicant` object in the code. Note that the `Applicant` object is a custom Java object. We need to add it to the class path. Hence, for doing so, we add JARs to the workflow. We have seen how to do so in *Chapter 1, Installing and Getting Started with Bonita*. We can package our custom Java classes into a JAR file and add this JAR file to the workflow. Click on the **Extensions** menu and choose the **Add/Remove JAR files** option. Here we can browse for the JAR file on the system and add it to the workflow. Thereafter, the class path will be updated with our custom Java classes, too.

Next, while defining the **Drools** connector, click on **Edit expression...** and enter the following code:

```
import com.company.entities.Applicant;
Applicant applicant = new Applicant();
ArrayList list = new ArrayList();
list.add(applicant);
return list;
```

Click on **OK** to return to the previous screen.

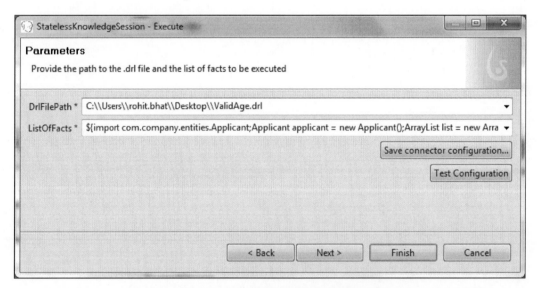

Figure 5.5: Executing the Drools connector in Bonita

When we click on the **Next** button, we are taken to a screen where we can map the output of the connector to a variable, either a pool variable or a step variable. Note that the output variable is stored in a list of objects called **revisedListOfFacts**. The drools engine runs the input list that we specified earlier and modifies the object within the list. It returns the array list with the modified object.

If we click on the drop-down option, then we can see the methods associated with the list of objects. We can also edit the expression in Groovy. Type the following code in Groovy:

```
import com.company.entities.Applicant;
return (Applicant)revisedListOfFacts.get(0);
```

As **revisedListOfFacts** is an array list, we get the first element from it. The type of the object is `Applicant`, so we cast it and return the object.

In the **Destination variable** field, we select a process variable of the Java type **Applicant**. This destination variable can be created at this step, too.

Thus, we saw how to run the **Drools** connector and modify objects.

We can also use the other **Drools** connector depending on the need, but the most useful one would be the one that we are seeing right now. Drools is a simple way of implementing any kind of business logic. In fact, an Excel sheet containing business logic can easily be converted into a drools file via code. Try doing that yourself as a task.

Database connectors

One of the most important connectors is the **Database** connector in Bonita. Quite often, we have to pool data from an external database or write to an external database for persistence. This database would be different than the databases used by Bonita internally for persistence. Bonita saves the state of the workflow after each step in an internal database. All the variables and values, plus a plethora of references are stored by Bonita internally at each step in the workflow. But there may be cases where we need to either extract data from an external database to be shown in the workflow, or write to an external database for our own purpose.

Bonita provides a lot of **Database** connectors to achieve this functionality. Connectors for most of the commonly used databases globally are already defined by Bonita. We have options to choose between JDBC, Access, DB2, H2, HSQL, MS SQL Server, MySQL, Oracle, PostgreSQL, and others.

Let us define a MySQL database connection. In our **TicketingWorkflow** process, we need to fetch the data of the flights. This information will be retrieved from the database. This is one of the uses of a **Database** connector in Bonita where the information is fetched from an external source. Let us set up a MySQL database on our local machine. We need to create a database called **TicketingWorkflow**, which will contain all the tables required for making the booking.

Adding Connectors

Click on the **BookTickets** step, add a MySQL connector, and call it `GetFlights`. Make sure that it is at the finish event of the step. Fill in the database information in the next screen as shown in the following screenshot or as per the database parameters you might be using:

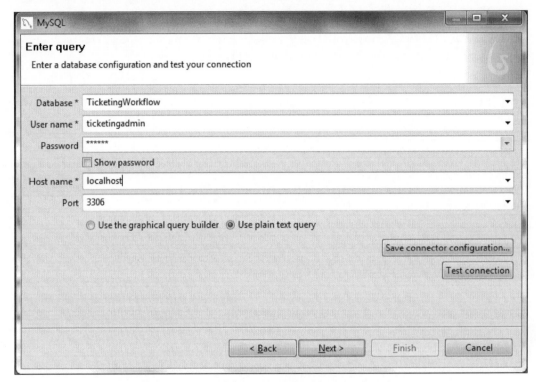

Figure 5.6 : Configuring the MySQL Database connector

We have to enter the query in the next screen. Note that this query has to be entered without the `${}` parameter that encapsulates a Groovy text. But if we have to use the process data or variables, we can indeed use `${}` and write Groovy script inside the curly braces.

It is always better to write the SQL query in a text editing tool and then paste it in Bonita. Write the following SQL query and enter it in the query section:

```
SELECT A.FROM_LOCATION, A.TO_LOCATION, B.AIRLINE,
  B.LOGO_FILE_PATH, TIME_FORMAT(B.DEPARTURE, '%H:%I'),
  TIME_FORMAT(B.ARRIVAL, '%H:%I'), TIME_FORMAT(B.DURATION,
  '%H:%I'), B.PRICE FROM TRAVEL_INFORMATION A, FLIGHT_INFORMATION
  B WHERE A.FROM_LOCATION='${from}' AND A.TO_LOCATION='${to}' AND
  A.FLIGHT_ID=B.FLIGHT_ID;
```

[84]

We are selecting certain fields from two tables by performing a join on them. In addition, we are also displaying the time in a particular format, namely HH:MM. We need this format to display the departure, arrival, and duration of the flight.

The database schema has been given in the *Appendix, Deploying Bonita on a Server*. You can also access the files by clicking on the following links:

- DDL for database: `http://textsave.de/6SJ`
- DML: http://textsave.de/7SJ

Just copy the text and run it in a query editor of any SQL.

Now, click on the **Next** button and we can see that the result is stored in the `rowSet` variable. Note that this `rowSet` is different from the Java `rowSet`. Although functionally similar, this `rowSet` is serializable, while Java's `rowSet` isn't. Let us save this `rowSet` in a pool variable of the Java object type `rowSet` (`org.bonitasoft.connectors.database.RowSet`). We will utilize this `rowSet` for populating various fields in the next form, that is, **Choose Flights**.

Groovy scripting

At times, we might have to use Groovy scripts in the form of connectors. These scripts can be run at the start or at the end of a particular step. This Groovy scripting connector is exactly similar to the Groovy scripts we have written before. You can check out the groovy example page here:

`http://groovy.codehaus.org/Cookbook+Examples`

Other connectors

There are a lot of connectors available for use in Bonita. We have explored some of them. If you want to have a look at the other connectors available in Bonita, then check out the official connectors guide here:

`http://www.bonitasoft.com/node/5619`

Finalizing the web form data

We have seen how the connectors work in Bonita. Now we need to edit certain fields in the forms that we had left empty before as we didn't have the data with us. Now, as we have learned how to use connectors, we have all the necessary data. Let us finalize these forms now.

We have obtained the data from the database connector and saved it in the `rowSet` variable. Now, we need to populate the fields of the `ChooseFlight` form using this data.

Open the **ChooseFlight** web form and populate each field as follows:

- **The Image widget**: The label of this widget should contain the name of the airline. Hence, click on **Edit expression...** for the label and enter the following:

    `rowSet.toList(3).get(0);`

    `rowSet` contains the result set of the SQL query. Hence, we extract the third column of the result set, which is the airline name according to the SQL query that we have written. This will give a list of all the airline names that match the SQL query. Out of this list, we extract the first element with the `get(0)` method.

    Similarly, in the **Data** field of the **Image** widget, enter the following:

    `rowSet.toList(4).get(0);`

    Here, we get the fourth column of the result set, which is the file path of the logo for the particular airline.

- **The Departure widget**: In the **Departure** widget field, we have to display the time of departure of the flight in HH:MM format. We get this format directly from the database with the SQL query we wrote before. Enter the following code in the **Data** field of the **Departure** widget:

    `rowSet.toList(5).get(0);`

- **The Arrival widget**: Enter the following code in the **Data** section:

    `rowSet.toList(6).get(0);`

- **The Duration widget**: Similarly, we get the duration from the `rowSet` column:

    `rowSet.toList(6).get(0);`

- **Price**: We get the price for an individual ticket from the database. But we have to multiply it by the number of passengers. Hence, we enter the following code in the **Data** section of the **Price** widget:

  ```
  return "\$" +
    Double.valueOf(rowSet.toList(8).get(0))*Double.valueOf
    (passengerNumber);
  ```

  We are returning the price in dollars. But in the Groovy expression, we have to escape the $ sign, as the $ sign is used in regular expressions to denote the end of a line.

Now, let us run the process and see how the information is displayed in the ChooseFlight step. Let us select a single way flight from London to Delhi with two passengers. Choose any date. The information in the **ChooseFlight** steps is displayed as given:

Figure 5.7: Displaying flight information to the user

The spacing and placement of widgets in this form doesn't look too good as this is the default placement and we haven't changed any properties of the fields. We will learn how to change the appearance of the widgets in *Chapter 7, Customizing Look and Feel*. Here, we just focus on the functionality of the form.

Hence, we have now seen how to populate the widget data from various types of connectors. These connectors are of the utmost use in displaying and exporting data from the workflow.

Summary

In this section, we visited the various connectors that are provided by Bonita. In a nutshell, Bonita connectors are used to get data into the workflow or externalize the data from the workflow. All these connectors can be implemented by the various APIs of the tasks that we want to perform. These APIs have to be coded in Java or Groovy. But Bonita has added a layer of abstraction on these APIs and we just have to configure the various connectors that are provided. These connectors are more than enough to get the majority of tasks done. We have seen how the **Bonita** connectors, **Email** connectors, **Database** connectors, and **Groovy** connectors work with an example. Similarly there are other connectors that we can explore, depending on the functionality we wish to achieve. There are even some connectors that have been contributed by the community and are available for use on the Bonitasoft portal. You can check them out at `http://www.bonitasoft.org/exchange/index.php`. Make use of these powerful connectors to increase the functionality of your workflow. In the next chapter, we will have a look at methods to configure page flow, customizing the way the inbox looks, and how to externalize web forms. In addition, we will also learn about the ways inbox parameters can be configured from the Bonita Studio.

6
Configuring the Page Flow

By now, we have learned how to model processes, create web forms, and use connectors for data flow. In this chapter, we will explore the inbox view of Bonita and also learn how to configure the entry, view and overview page flow, the status of a case in the inbox as well as a way to externalize the forms, and how to pass parameters to the external form. This is essential in how the end user perceives the application. By various degrees of customization, we can improve the overall user experience.

Configuring the Page Flow

The inbox view

Let us start with some customization of the inbox. In the initial chapters, we have already seen some administrative tasks associated with the inbox. The inbox is the landing page for any user. It lists the tasks that are currently pending for the user to complete, the tasks the user has worked on, and so on. Here, we will have a look at the other options available in the inbox view. Run the **Ticketing Workflow** application and, when the **Welcome** form appears, go back to the **Inbox**. Here we can see that there is one item pending in the inbox, which is the case we just started. Click on the case and a details page opens up. Here we have the options to look at the form, attachments, comments, and history.

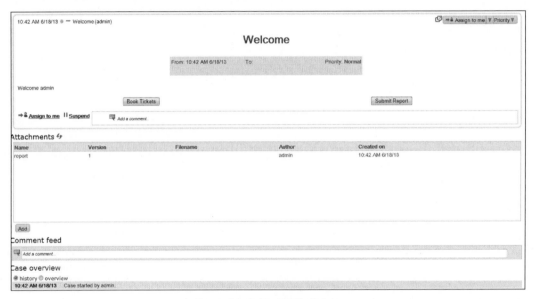

Figure 6.1: Inbox detailed view

In the topmost section, we have the form view. Here, we have an option to open the form in a new tab in a full screen mode. Also, we have an assignee option on the top-right corner. It might so happen that a case might be in your inbox, but you might not have the time to go over it. Hence, you can just assign it to someone else so that it lands in his or her inbox. Let us look at the steps to do so:

1. If you click on the down arrow next to **Assign to me**, you will find an option to assign the task to some other user. Here we have to enter the username of the person we want to assign the task to. In the list of available candidates, we can choose to remove the current user. This will assign the current case to the new user and remove the case from the inbox of the current user.

Figure 6.2: Assign a case to another user

2. After you click on **Apply**, the case disappears from the inbox of the current user. Let us log in via `jerry` and see that the case is now present in his inbox.

3. We will move forward with the workflow via the submit report route. After you click on **Submit Report**, this case will no longer be available in jerry's inbox. Jerry was made the actor only for the **Welcome** step and not the next step, which is **Report Number**. As the actor of the **Report Number** step is the initiator, which is the admin in this case, the **Report Number** step lands in the admin's inbox. Thus, we need to log in using the admin's credentials.

4. Select **2** as the number of reports and click on **Next**.

5. Upload a report and click on the next step. We are taken to the download report step. Here, click on the next step.

6. Go back to the **Inbox**. We can see that there is an item in the inbox called **Submit that is pending**. This is the second report that we have to submit. Click on the case and you will be able to see the details of the case.

Configuring the Page Flow

Let us have a look at the other sections of the inbox. Beneath the form, there is an attachment section. This section contains the default attachments process variables and their details. Any kind of attachment that has been associated with a step is available in this section. It stores all the attachments available for use at this step. Next up, we have the comments section. Here, every user can input his or her comments while executing the task and the comments will be visible at the later steps, too. Beneath that, we have the case overview section. Here, there are two options: the history and the overview. The history is a step-by-step account of the details of each step of the pool. It has information about who started the step at what time and a summary of the step. The overview contains information about all the variables in a particular pool. If we click on each individual item in the history, we can see the value of the variables at each step. The variables that are shown are the pool variables. We can see that the value of count has changed from the **Welcome** step to the **ReportNumber** step. This is the default history page that is shown at each step. But we would be able to glean more information about the history page if we show the values that were filled in at each step. For this purpose, we would be creating the history page for each of the steps in the workflow.

Entry, view, and overview page flow

The entry, view, and overview page forms are available either for the entire pool or for individual steps. Let us have a look at how to configure these page flows:

1. Click on the **Welcome** step. In the **Application** tab, we can see that there are three subtabs: the **Entry Pageflow**, the **View Pageflow**, and the **Confirmation** message. The **Entry Pageflow** subtab contains the Web forms that we previously defined. The **Confirmation** message contains the message that is displayed at the end of submitting the form if the next step isn't performed by the current user. If the next step is also performed by the current user, then the flow goes directly to the next step without the confirmation message. The **View Pageflow** is where we can define the form to be shown when the history is loaded.

2. Click on the **View Pageflow** tab and add a form. In the option to create a new form, select the radio button to duplicate the form from a list. Here, you will be able to see all the forms of all the processes that have been imported into the Studio.

3. Click on the **+** button next to **TicketPurchase**. We can now see all the forms that are available in this pool. Select the **Welcome** step, change the name if you wish to, and click on **Finish**.

4. Next, let's make the history form for the **ReportNumber** step. Here, we create the history form by duplicating the **ReportNumber** form. Note that all the form fields in **View Pageflow** will be non-editable. In this form, we can see that the **ReportNumberOptions** field is prepopulated with the data. But the initial value of the field should be changed.
5. In the **Entry Pageflow** tab, we would have saved the radio button option in the variable count. Hence, in the history page for this step, the initial value can be set to count as it makes sense to have the previously saved value in the data for the history form.
6. Change the initial value to count in the **ReportNumberOptions** field in the history page.
7. Similarly, create the history form for the **Submit Report** and the **Download Report** forms. Make sure that the initial value of all fields is the variable that the value is saved to in the entry form.
8. Now, run the process again and trace the same steps we did before. If we look at the history form now, we see the following:

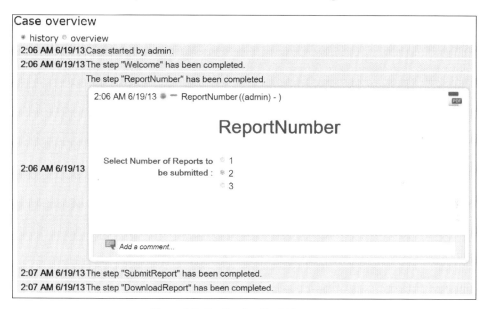

Figure 6.3: Configuring the history page

We can create the history page for each step in this manner, thereby overriding the default behavior of the history page and introducing our own page. Similarly, the overview page, by default, provides the value of all the process variables. We can change this page by clicking on the pool and, in the **Applications** tab, selecting **View Pageflow**. Here, we can define a page flow similar to how we define a history page.

User XP options in Studio

From Bonita Studio, we have certain parameters that we can set for defining the User XP. Let us start with the pool customization. Click on any pool and select the **UserXP** tab. Here, we see an option to add categories. Categories are displayed in the inbox for each case of the particular pool. Select the **TicketPurchase** pool and add the category `Ticket Purchase`.

Next, we can specify additional parameters to be displayed in the User XP for each step. Thus, click on the **Welcome** step and navigate to the **UserXP** tab. Here, we can specify the **Dynamic title**, **Dynamic Description**, **Step Summary**, and **Estimated execution time** fields. A normal title, consisting of the step title, is displayed in the User XP by default. If we want to change this, or input some dynamic label, we can set it up in **Dynamic title**. Similarly, we can specify the description that is displayed along with the title. The **Step Summary** field is the text that is displayed in the history page. The **Estimated execution time** field is used to categorize tasks into "at risk" or "overdue".

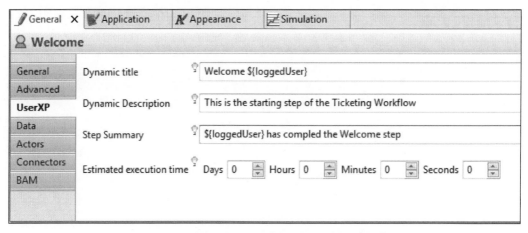

Figure 6.4: Editing the UserXP elements in Bonita Studio

Now, if we want to see the changes that have taken place in the **UserXP** tab, click on **Run**. After you go to the inbox, you can see something similar to the following screenshot:

Figure 6.5: Changing the User XP

We can see that the **Ticket Purchase** category is present next to the label titled **Inbox**. Also, we can see that the dynamic title states **Welcome admin**. The dynamic description is displayed next to the title. Now, complete the **Welcome** step and check the history of the step.

Figure 6.6: Changed step summary in the history view

Process status in User XP

We can also change the way Bonita Engine assigns the case number to each individual case. For this, we need to log in using the admin view. Click on the **Process** tab in the left-hand column. In the list of processes available, click on any process. The details panel opens up. Here, we can define the process related parameters. The first parameter we see is about the form application. As we have created custom web forms, they are referenced as external form applications. In the **Description** section, we can customize the description of the cases displayed in the inbox. Here, we can use certain variables provided by Bonita, namely `process.name`, `case.indexNumber`, `case.initiator`, `case.startDate`, and `case.currentState`. By default, `process.name+ - #+case.indexNumber` is shown. Let us change it to `process.name+ #+case.indexNumber+ #+case.initiator`.

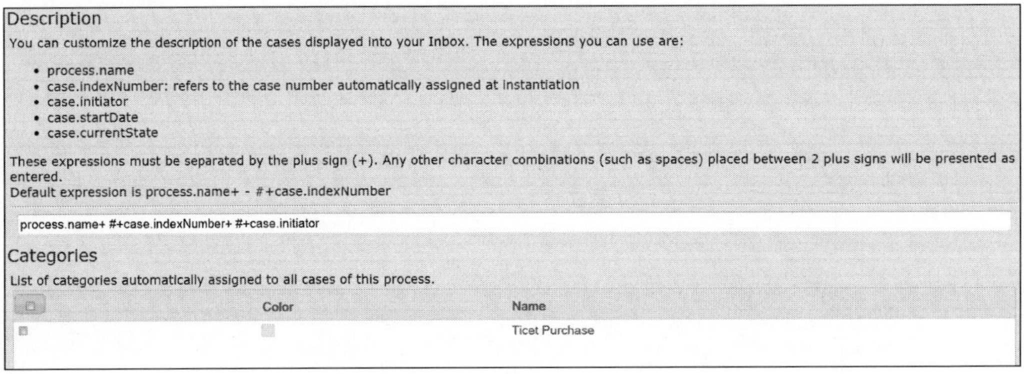

Figure 6.7: Changing the process description

Externalizing forms

Apart from creating forms inside Bonita Studio, we are also given the option of externalizing forms. This option is only available in the Subscription Pack version, not in the Community Version. However, we shall see the usefulness of this feature here. We can create our own forms outside the studio and integrate them in the workflow. For each step in the workflow, we can point the entry page flow to an external URL where we would be defining our forms. We need to make sure that our forms serve the correct information according to the case. For this reason, we can pass the process instance and the activity instance from the Bonita Engine to the external forms. We can then make use of APIs to set parameters and run connectors from the external forms.

Each web form of each case can be identified by two parameters: the process instance UUID and the activity instance UUID. These parameters are received from the Studio by making use of the Bonita variables from the Groovy editor. Let us make our workflow point to an external form instead of the inbuilt web form.

Click on the **Welcome** step and, in the **Application** tab, select the **Entry Pageflow** tab. Here, click on the **Redirect to URL** radio button. In the Groovy editor, enter the following code:

```
return
   "http://localhost:8080/Welcome.html?processUUID=
   "+processInstance.getUUID().getValue()+"&activityUUID=
   "+activityInstance.getUUID().getValue();
```

Here, we assume that we have a page called **Welcome.html** in our ROOT folder of TOMCAT. The GET request parameters have the processUUID and the activityUUID by which the step is defined. In addition, check the box for defining the return URL as a parameter. This appends the URL with the submitURL, which is the URL to go to on submission of the form. If we hit this URL after the form is submitted, then Bonita assumes that the step is completed and moves forward to the next step. Also, we can return the value of any field from the form as a GET parameter. Here, we return the parameter submit and save it in the variable nextStep. Thus, the externalization of the form looks something like this:

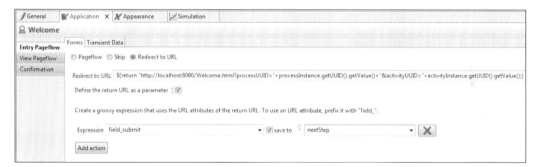

Figure 6.8: Redirecting to an external URL from Bonita Studio

Now the next task is to create the HTML page. We won't be creating it here, but it is fairly simple to do so. We can even adopt the MVC architecture to serve the external pages. It is up to us how we do it.

Summary

In this section, we have seen how to configure the User XP of the Bonita inbox. We can customize a lot of parameters that have a direct bearing on the appearance of the inbox. We have also seen how to get the detailed view of any particular case in the inbox and we have also seen the history pages and overview pages. In addition, we have also learned how to externalize the Web forms, instead of creating them from inside Bonita. In the next chapter, we will have a look at the customizations of the look and feel of the application, as well as the customization of the User XP in terms of visual representation.

7
Customizing Look and Feel

In the previous chapter, we looked at how we can configure the page flow inside Bonita. We had a look at the history and overview pages, and also learned about externalizing the Web forms. In this chapter, we will learn about customizing the look and feel of the Web forms inside the Studio and also of the inbox view. In addition, we will have a look at the other appearance options that are available for customization. Note that the **Look'n'feel** editor is available only in the Subscription Pack version. However, the CSS and other properties can be changed in the Community Edition, too. But for completely changing the **Look'n'feel** properties, the Subscription Pack is needed.

Customizing web forms

Open the **TicketingWorkflow** process and open the Web form of the **BookTicket** step. Let us have a look at the customization options available to us at the form level in Bonita. Click on the **TripOptions** radio button. Here, we can specify the look and feel of these options in the **Appearance** tab. We get the options to modify the grid, cell, items, label, and field elements. For each of these components, we can change the text styles.

Let us look at each of these elements individually:

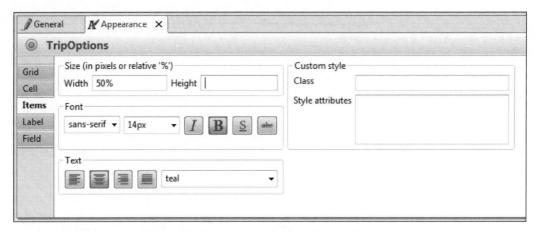

Figure 7.1: Customizing different fields of web forms

- **Grid**: For the grid element, we can specify the height and width of the grid, either absolutely in pixels or relatively in percentage.
- **Cell**: In the cell element, in addition to specifying the height and width of the cell, we can also enter the class of our custom css file. We have to include this custom file and mention the name of the class present in the css file. Also, we can specify the css style attributes.
- **Items**: The items style indicates the individual items of the radio options. Here, we can specify the height and width of the items, define our own custom style, and mention style attributes. In addition, we can also specify the font style, font size, and font attributes. Also, we can customize the text alignment and color of the text. These options give us control over the various form elements.
- **Label**: In addition to all the attributes present in the **Items** options, the **Label** attribute also contains the option to specify the label of the radio options relative to the options.
- **Field**: The **Field** options are similar to the **Items** options.

These various elements can differ based on the widget we choose to customize; for example, the **Select** box doesn't have an **Items** option, while the **Submit** button doesn't have the **Items** as well as the **Label** options. Thus, we can customize various web form fields. Next, let us have a look at how to change the look and feel of all the forms together.

Changing Look'n'feel

Click on any pool and navigate to the **Application** tab. Here, after selecting the **Look'n'feel** tab, we can click on **Apply a look'n'feel**. Bonita gives certain default templates for **Look'n'feel**. We can even import our own **Look'n'feel** here. The default **Look'n'feel** have a preview image that can help us gauge how the template might look like.

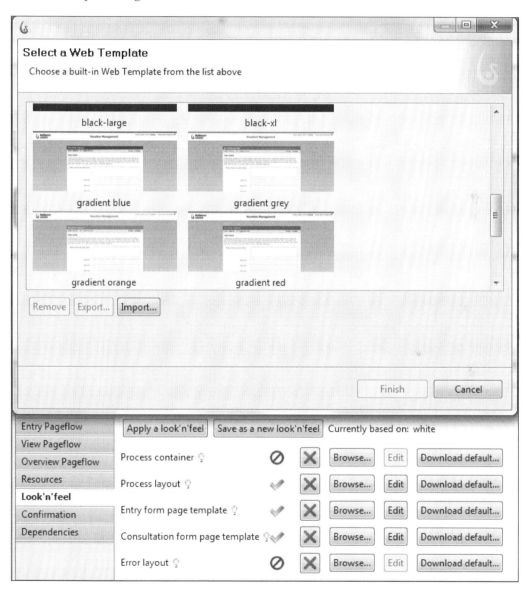

Figure 7.2: Applying a Look'n'feel resource

Customizing Look and Feel

For a detailed view of the **Look'n'feel**, you can even apply it and run the application to check the various styling elements. Note that if you apply a new **Look'n'feel**, you lose all the information that you might have previously edited.

A **Look'n'feel** resource has five templates for various style elements:

- **Process container**: This template is used to add styling elements and JavaScript around the process layout and related resources.
- **Process layout**: This is the template used for laying out the process. The process layout includes the top header of the Web page and links for logging out, inbox navigation, and so on.
- **Entry form page template**: This is the template of the Web form in Bonita. The styling of the form can be controlled by this template.
- **Consultation form page template**: The view page of a web form is generated using this particular template. For changing the history page of a form, we can edit this template.
- **Error layout**: If we have to display an error message, we can make use of this template.

These templates are HTML pages and we can either edit them or replace them with our own custom HTML templates. We can also disable or enable a template by toggling between the buttons next to the template.

Adding Resources to the workflow

In addition to customizing the look and feel of the workflow, we can also add custom CSS and other resources, such as images, to enhance the styling of the Web forms. A `Resources` folder is created when a new workflow diagram is created. It contains an `application` folder, which in turn contains two folders: `css` and `images`. We can also add custom files and folders to the resources so that they are available for use throughout the applications.

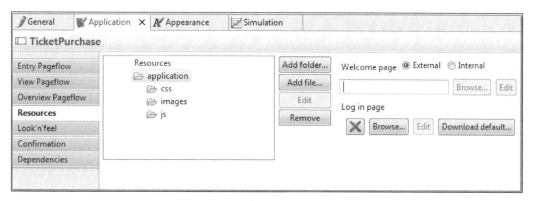

Figure 7.3: Adding Resources files

A good practice is to add all the JavaScript files in a separate `js` folder within the `application` folder. Similarly, we can add additional custom images and css files, too. We can also change the login page from this console. We can override the default Bonita login page or even make changes to it depending on our requirement.

Application Look'n'feel

The option of editing a particular **Look'n'feel** template is available only in the Subscription Pack version of Bonita Open Solution. Editing a **Look'n'feel** template is made pretty easy with the editor provided by Bonita. Let us have a look at the way to create a new **Look'n'feel** and edit it.

Click on the **Look'n'feel** menu button and select **New**. Here, we can define a new Look'n'feel by selecting existing elements as templates. We have much more options to choose from in the Subscription Pack compared to the Community Edition while applying **Look'n'feel** to a form.

Customizing Look and Feel

Note that we can edit the **Look'n'feel** for forms as well as the User Experience. Select the white application template as it is a broad form that would be useful in displaying the elements of our form in a better manner. Name the new Look'n'feel and select **Create**. This opens up the Look'n'feel editor.

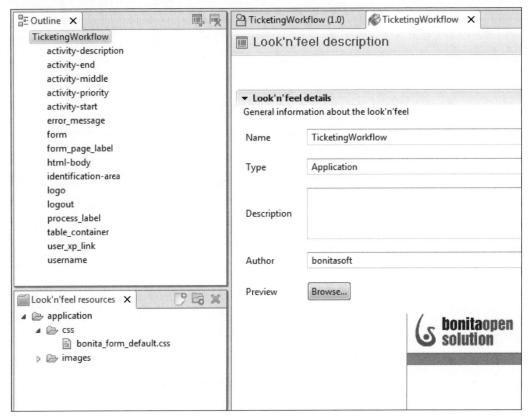

Figure 7.4: The Look'n'feel editor in Bonitasoft

Here, the left-hand panel has all the attributes of this particular Look'n'feel, such as the **form**, **logo**, **process_label**, and **error_message**. Clicking on each element opens up the editor in the right-hand pane. The right-hand pane has various HTML attributes associated with a particular element.

Let us explore the HTML attributes further. Click on any of the elements in the left-hand panel, for example, **form**. The rand-hand panel contains details about this particular element. The **form** element is used to display the form area on the Web page. The default css file associated with this form is mentioned, as well as the `css div` file that would be used.

We can override the CSS with the other sections available in the right-hand panel. Let us change the text properties. We can set the **Font family** field to **Calibri** and change the default text color. You can tweak the CSS properties in an easy manner using the Bonitasoft editor.

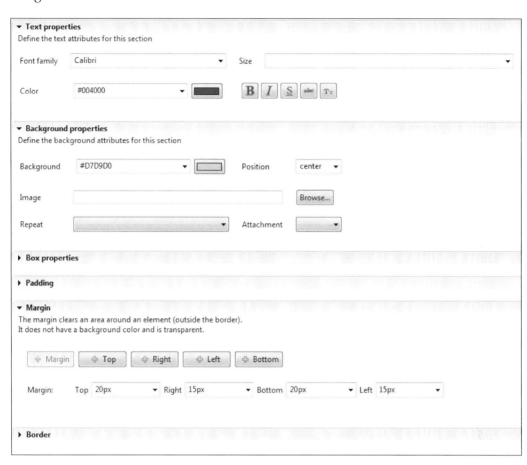

Figure 7.5: Editing CSS properties using the Bonitasoft Look'n'feel editor

We can also change or edit the CSS property directly. Note that whatever change you make in the editor, it gets reflected in the css file. If you want to use your own css file, you have to add it to the **Look'n'feel** resources panel on the bottom left. You can change the **logo** and other CSS properties. You can also preview the changes you have made by clicking on the **Preview** button in the **Application** menu bar.

You can add certain preview options; select the form to preview and other elements before Bonita generates the preview for you.

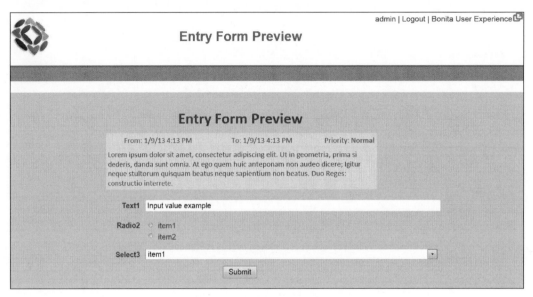

Figure 7.6: Look'n'feel preview

Thus we can play around with the HTML and CSS properties of the forms and change them according to our needs. This feature is only available in the Subscription Pack of Bonitasoft, though.

User Experience Look'n'feel

In addition to changing the styling of the Web forms, we can also customize the User Experience Inbox view of Bonitasoft. This inbox view again has the HTML and CSS files that you can edit. You can also add certain JavaScript elements to the User Experience console. Let us have a look at the way to create a new User Experience Look'n'feel.

Similarly for creating a new **Look'n'feel** resource for the Web form, when we click on **New** in the **Look'n'feel** menu item, choose the default **UserXP** to edit. Here, in addition to the elements present in the left-hand panel for the various sections of the User Experience, there are two HTML pages, called **BonitaConsole.html** and **admin.html**. The **BonitaConsole.html** page contains the HTML code of the **User Inbox** page. The administration page code is contained in **admin.html**. In these two HTML pages, we can add our own HTML or menu items or buttons to customize the inbox.

The css files contain the styling elements for displaying the Bonita forms, and also the styling of the inbox elements. We can also change the CSS with the provided editor if we do not want to edit the CSS code directly. Let us change the inbox colors and gradient just to see how that is reflected in the final design.

Click on the **Bonita User Experience** element and change the background color in the background properties. You can also play around with other aspects of the **Bonita User Experience** to suit your needs.

Let us also see how we can add a menu item to User Experience and include a style in the css file, too. Open up **BonitaConsole.html**, locate the `div` with ID as `"bos_top_right_links"`, and add another span element titled `Search`. We can redirect the user to a custom page when he/she clicks on **Search**. However, for the time being, let us redirect the user to Google search. This is how the `div` will look after you've made the changes:

```
<div id="bos_top_right_links" class="bos_float_right">
<span id="user_id"></span>
<span id="bos_locale_chooser"></span>
<span id="bos_user_preferences"></span>
<span class="identif-2">|</span>
<span id="bos_about"></span>
<span id="ui_mode_selector_parent" class="bos_empty_menu">
<span class="identif-2">|</span>
<span onclick="window.location = 'homepage?ui=admin&' +
getParams(window.location.href, false)" class="identif-2" id="ui_mode_
selector"></span>
<span onclick="window.location = 'http://google.com'" class="custom">
| Search</span>
</span>
<span id="bos_logout_parent" class="bos_empty_menu">
<span class="identif-2">|</span>
<span id="bos_logout"></span>
</span>
</div>
```

We have included a `span` element with the class `custom`. We will style the **Search** font via this custom CSS class. Include the following piece of code in a new file called `custom.css`:

```
/** Custom CSS */
.custom {
  font-family: arial, sans-serif;
  font-size: 10px
}
```

Customizing Look and Feel

Add this file to the css folder via the **Add file** button present on the left-hand bottom panel of the **Look'n'feel** editor. Now we need to include this file in the **BonitaConsole.html** page so that the HTML page can refer to our custom CSS code. Include the following line inside the `<head>` tag of the HTML:

```
<link type="text/css" rel="stylesheet" href="css/custom.css"/>
```

Here, we are just adding a link for **Search** with some custom CSS code. Similarly, you can add or edit the entire page, as the HTML and CSS are available to be modified. We can preview all our changes by clicking on the **Preview** button.

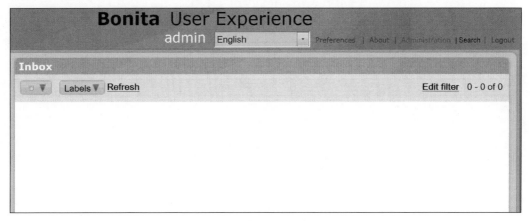

Figure 7.7: Customizing the User Experience

We can see that there is a **Search** menu item next to the **Administration** button on the top-right bar of the **Bonita User Experience** page.

Thus, there are a lot of customizations possible in the User Experience as well as the form elements in Bonita. The default design can be drastically changed by tinkering around with the HTML and CSS properties.

Summary

We have seen the way to customize the **Look'n'feel** resources in Bonita. We have created a new Look'n'feel resource for the application form as well as for the User Experience. In addition, we have also learned about the styling of various form elements. Thus, we have learned the various elements that can be customized to redesign our forms and the User Experience.

With this, we have finally come to the end of developing applications with Bonita Open Solution. Along the way, we have learned various functionalities that this tool provides us to develop a Business Process Model and also to develop a Workflow application. However, we will also learn how to deploy the application on a server in the *Appendix, Deploying Bonita on a Server*.

Deploying Bonita on a Server

By now, we have seen how to develop applications in Bonita Open Solution by leveraging the ease of the Studio and the power of the Execution Engine. The next step for creating any application is to deploy it on a server so that the end users can access it and utilize the application for their purposes. We will deploy Bonita Open Solution 5.10 on a Tomcat 6.0.35 server.

Downloading the Tomcat bundle

Bonitasoft has bundled the Execution engine along with a Tomcat 6.0.35 bundle. The advantage of using this bundle is that the entire Bonita Execution Engine is packaged and deployed as an application in Tomcat. We have the ability to change the various parameters, such as databases used from this bundle. We can also deploy other apps through a war file in Tomcat. Thus, this Tomcat bundle is a customized bundle which incorporates Bonita Open Solution on top of a vanilla Tomcat installation.

You can download the Bonita Tomcat bundle from the following link:

`http://www.bonitasoft.com/products/download/other-versions-bos`

Click on **Version 5.10** and in the **Bundles** tab select the **Tomcat** bundle to download it. Unzip the file into a folder of your destination. Let's call the main folder of Tomcat as `TOMCAT_HOME`. If you explore the contents of the folder, you would find the default folders that are present in any vanilla Tomcat bundle. Let us now have a look at the various options available in this Tomcat bundle.

Exploring the Tomcat bundle

The TOMCAT_HOME folder has the following folders:

- bin: This binary folder includes all the executable and binary files, including the dll files necessary for Tomcat to run
- bonita: This folder contains the configuration files needed for the Bonita application, as well as storage for temporary files and the place where the default file-based database stores its files
- conf: This folder contains the configuration files for Tomcat as well as the Bonita configuration
- external: This folder contains the **Java Authentication and Authorization Service (JAAS)** configuration files
- lib: All the JAR files needed by Tomcat, Bonita, and other external applications are present in the lib folder
- logs: The Tomcat and Bonita logs are present in this folder
- temp: This folder is used as a temporary folder by **Java Virtual Machine (JVM)**
- webapps: All the webapps running on Tomcat are deployed in this directory
- work: This is a temporary working directory for web applications

The preceding are the main folders of Tomcat. However, we will get into the details of these shortly.

Starting and shutting Tomcat

You need Java installed to run Tomcat as it runs on a JVM. If you have JDK installed along with the JAVA_HOME environment variable, you're all set. In the bin folder, there are two executable files, startup.bat and shutdown.bat, for Windows and startup.sh and shutdown.sh for Linux. These bat commands and shell scripts are used to start and shut down the Tomcat server. While starting up Tomcat, the environment variables are checked and set in setenv.bat or setenv.sh. You can add your own environment variables by modifying this script.

Let us run startup.bat and see what happens. After you execute the file, the Tomcat server starts up and you would be able to see the status of the server. It deploys all the Web applications it has and then the server starts up. If you check the webapps folder, you will see two war files: bonita.war and bonita-app.war.

These are the application files that are required for Bonita Open Solution to run on Tomcat. The first time you start up, it will take some time as Tomcat explodes the war into different folders. Subsequent startups of Tomcat will not take as much time as these two files would have already been exploded.

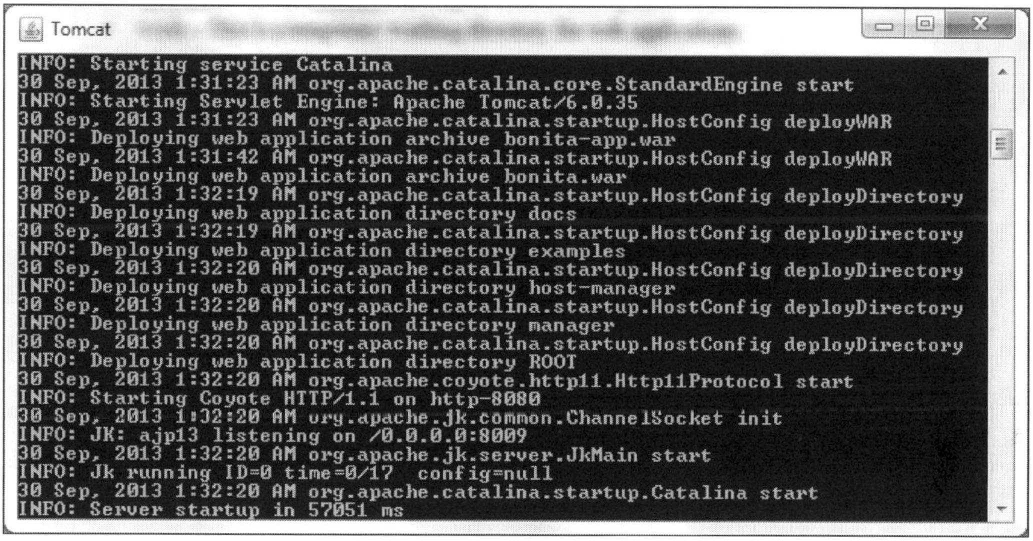

```
Tomcat
INFO: Starting service Catalina
30 Sep, 2013 1:31:23 AM org.apache.catalina.core.StandardEngine start
INFO: Starting Servlet Engine: Apache Tomcat/6.0.35
30 Sep, 2013 1:31:23 AM org.apache.catalina.startup.HostConfig deployWAR
INFO: Deploying web application archive bonita-app.war
30 Sep, 2013 1:31:42 AM org.apache.catalina.startup.HostConfig deployWAR
INFO: Deploying web application archive bonita.war
30 Sep, 2013 1:32:19 AM org.apache.catalina.startup.HostConfig deployDirectory
INFO: Deploying web application directory docs
30 Sep, 2013 1:32:19 AM org.apache.catalina.startup.HostConfig deployDirectory
INFO: Deploying web application directory examples
30 Sep, 2013 1:32:20 AM org.apache.catalina.startup.HostConfig deployDirectory
INFO: Deploying web application directory host-manager
30 Sep, 2013 1:32:20 AM org.apache.catalina.startup.HostConfig deployDirectory
INFO: Deploying web application directory manager
30 Sep, 2013 1:32:20 AM org.apache.catalina.startup.HostConfig deployDirectory
INFO: Deploying web application directory ROOT
30 Sep, 2013 1:32:20 AM org.apache.coyote.http11.Http11Protocol start
INFO: Starting Coyote HTTP/1.1 on http-8080
30 Sep, 2013 1:32:20 AM org.apache.jk.common.ChannelSocket init
INFO: JK: ajp13 listening on /0.0.0.0:8009
30 Sep, 2013 1:32:20 AM org.apache.jk.server.JkMain start
INFO: Jk running ID=0 time=0/17  config=null
30 Sep, 2013 1:32:20 AM org.apache.catalina.startup.Catalina start
INFO: Server startup in 57051 ms
```

Figure 8.1: Starting Tomcat 6.0.35

Open up your browser and hit `http://localhost:8080/`. 8080 is the default port that is specified in the bundle. We will look at how to change this port later. The default Tomcat page opens up. You can read the information specified on this page as well as look at the examples provided by Tomcat if you're not familiar with servlets and JSPs.

Now, let us have a look at the Bonita application. The Bonita application was exploded in the `Bonita` folder. Hence, to access it, we need to hit `http://localhost:8080/bonita`. You will be redirected to a Bonita login page, the same page that you encounter when you log out of the Bonita studio while running the User Experience. Here, enter the admin credentials of admin and click on **Log in**. You will now be able to view the User Experience of Bonita. This User Experience is similar to the one that was available with Bonita Studio.

Customizing database connections

By default, Bonita Open Solution uses the file-based h2 database for its internal operations. Let us look at the places where this is configured and also change the connections to make sure that it uses MySQL instead. This practice will allow us to learn about the configurations files as well as setting up our MySQL server as Bonita's internal database.

In the `TOMCAT_HOME` folder, open up the `conf` folder. Here, you will find the Tomcat configuration files as well as the database files for Bonita. Let us now look at the internal database used by Bonita. Open up the file `context.xml` in any editing tool, such as Sublime Text. In this file, we can see that the default datasource is the one used by the h2 database. Beneath that, there is a commented datasource to be used for MySQL. Let us comment the h2 datasource and uncomment the MySQL datasource. We need to change a few parameters for the MySQL datasource, too.

> The way to comment in an XML file is to include the comment text commented within a `<!--` opening tag and a `-->` closing tag.

- There are two databases that Bonita uses internally for all its purposes. One is called `bonita journal` and one is `bonita history`.
- Firstly, we need to change the username and password for the MySQL server that we would be using. In the **Username** and **password** fields, enter your MySQL username and password.
- MySQL uses port 3306 by default, and the default names for the databases used are `bonita_journal` and `bonita_history`. You can change this in the URL parameter of both the datasources. Create the two databases that you mentioned in the URL parameter in your MySQL server. You can let the other parameters remain the same.

This defines the data source that has to be used for Bonita. Now, we have to define the other database and hibernate properties, which we should do in two other files. These are the `bonita-journal.properties` and `bonita-history.properties` files present in the `TOMCAT_HOME/bonita/server/default/conf/` directory.

Open the `bonita-journal.properties` file to find the different configurations for database access. The default database connections are made using the h2 database. This file has the other hibernate properties that are used to connect to the database. At the end of the file, there are commented sections that have the code for other databases. Let us uncomment the lines for MySQL, that is, line numbers 101 and 102.

The file now looks like the following code:

```
##
# MYSQL

hibernate.dialect
   org.hibernate.dialect.MySQL5InnoDBDialect
bonita.hibernate.interceptor
   org.ow2.bonita.env.interceptor.MySQLDescNullFirstInterceptor
```

Make sure that the `bonita.hibernate.interceptor` property and the value `MySQLDescNullFirstInterceptor` are on the same line. Now, we have uncommented the section for MySQL, so we need to comment out the sections for h2. Comment out the corresponding h2 database connection properties, found on lines 17 and 20.

You can leave the other properties unchanged; these are primarily hibernate properties. One property that you may change later is the property on line 23: `hibernate.hbm2ddl.auto`. This specifies that the tables required by Bonita should be created/updated as and when the database connection is made. This option is a must during the initial setup when the tables aren't set up, but it isn't needed later on when everything is up and running properly.

Make similar changes to the `bonita-history.properties` file. Now that we have changed all the properties, one thing that remains is the appropriate driver for MySQL. We have defined the driver `com.mysql.jdbc.Driver` in the `context.xml` file, but we do not know where to find this driver. Hence, we need to download the MySQL JAR that contains this driver class. We can download the latest MySQL Connector 5.0.8 from the following website:

http://dev.mysql.com/downloads/connector/j/

Download the platform-independent version and extract the zip file. You will find a JAR file, such as `mysql-connector-java-5.1.26-bin.jar` (the version may be different). Copy this jar into the `lib` folder of TOMCAT_HOME.

Deploying Bonita on a Server

Now run `startup.bat` from the `bin` folder of Tomcat. When you navigate to `http://localhost:8080/bonita`, you will have to log in using the admin credentials. The first time it will be slow, as all the required tables will be created in the database. Thereafter, you will be navigated to the user inbox.

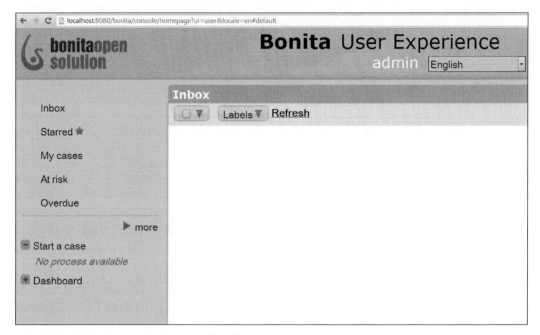

Figure 8.2: User Experience on the Tomcat server

 BOS SP users should copy their licenses to the `TOMCAT_HOME/bonita/server/licenses` folder for BOS SP Tomcat to work.

Logfiles

Log is an important part of troubleshooting and debugging. With the Tomcat container, there are various levels of log that can be set for different purposes. In the `TOMCAT_HOME/log` folder, you will find the following types of logs:

- Tomcat log: These are present in the files `catalina.log` and `localhost.log`. All the Tomcat engine logs are present in `catalina.log` and the virtual host that is configured by Tomcat, which is localhost, is present in the `localhost.log` file.

- Bonita log: The log generated by the Bonita Execution Engine are present in the `bonita.log` file. This contains the information related to every action that is done on the user experience.

The logging levels can be changed from the `logging.properties` files in the `TOMCAT_HOME/conf` folder.

Changing the configuration files

A lot of the Tomcat setup is customizable and is present in the `config` files. By changing these XML config files, we can change the behavior of Tomcat to suit our purpose. Let us first have a look at the Tomcat server config file and the various customizations.

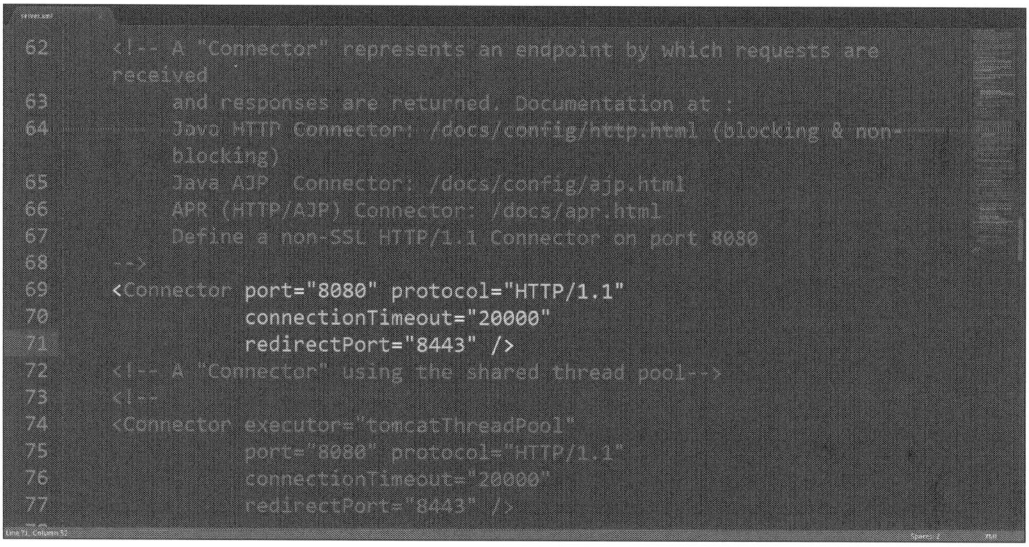

```
<!-- A "Connector" represents an endpoint by which requests are
     received
     and responses are returned. Documentation at :
     Java HTTP Connector: /docs/config/http.html (blocking & non-
     blocking)
     Java AJP  Connector: /docs/config/ajp.html
     APR (HTTP/AJP) Connector: /docs/apr.html
     Define a non-SSL HTTP/1.1 Connector on port 8080
-->
<Connector port="8080" protocol="HTTP/1.1"
           connectionTimeout="20000"
           redirectPort="8443" />
<!-- A "Connector" using the shared thread pool-->
<!--
<Connector executor="tomcatThreadPool"
           port="8080" protocol="HTTP/1.1"
           connectionTimeout="20000"
           redirectPort="8443" />
```

Figure 8.3: Tomcat server configuration file

Here the connector for the HTTP/1.1 protocol is defined in the previous screenshot. We can change the port and also change the connection timeout, along with the other settings, such as the redirect port. A front-end Apache server can also be installed to work as a reverse proxy for Tomcat. You can read more about this at http://tomcat.apache.org/connectors-doc/generic_howto/proxy.html. In the commented code beneath, there is a connector for HTTP/1.1 over SSL. There is also a Valve defined for Bonita login. Bonita uses JAAS for logging in users.

Bonita login page

We have the ability to change the default login page of Bonita. Open the file `login.jsp` present in `TOMCAT_HOME/webapps/bonita/console`. Here, the HTML page can be modified to suit your purpose. I've changed the HTML page and here is how it looks after modification.

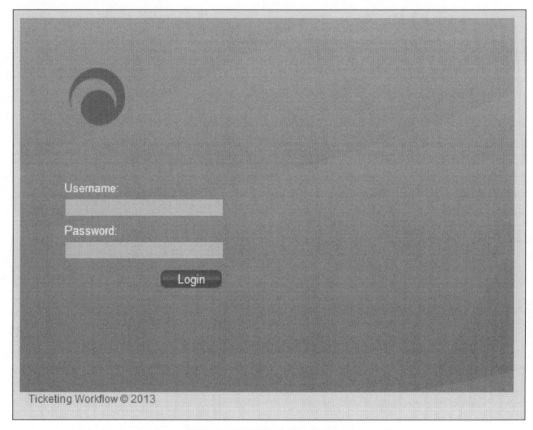

Figure 8.4: Modifying the login page

Here, only a basic modification is shown, but with HTML and Javascript/JQuery, the login page can be jazzed up a lot. We can integrate Bootstrap and other css classes, too.

Appendix

Bonita API and adding users into the database

If we're creating an application in Bonita that many users will use, then these users need to be created in Bonita and entered in the internal database. Often, it is quite possible that the user information is stored in a separate database. Manually adding those users into Bonita is a tedious task. Hence, we can create a separate application for this purpose that will be run only once: to input users into Bonita's internal database. For this purpose, we will leverage the Bonita APIs, which are useful in performing tasks with the Bonita Execution Engine. The Bonita APIs are Java-based and have extensive documentation here at `http://www.bonitasoft.org/docs/javadoc/bpm_engine/5.10/`.

Let us create a new process in Bonita Studio and use the Groovy editor to leverage these APIs. Let us have only two steps in the process, one to add roles and the other to add users to the database. The workflow should look like the following screenshot when completed:

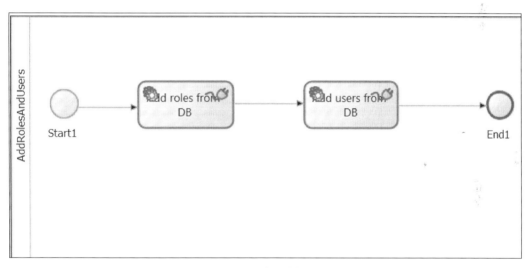

Figure 8.5: New process for adding roles and users

Deploying Bonita on a Server

In the **Add roles from DB** step, create a database connector, such as MySQL, enter the required information for connecting to it, and thereafter, enter the SQL query for selecting the role names.

Figure 8.6: MySQL connection properties

The SQL query might look something like this:

```
Select name
 from TICKETING_WORKFLOW.role
```

In the next step of the connector, where the connection output is meant to go to a destination variable, select **Edit expression...** in the connector output to bring up the Groovy editor.

Here, let us write the following piece of code to add a role with a particular name into Bonita:

```
import org.ow2.bonita.facade.IdentityAPI;
IdentityAPI identityAPI = apiAccessor.getIdentityAPI();
i=0;
// We have to iterate over each value that rowSet contains
rowSet.getValues().each {
  try {
    // We had selected the name of the role in the SQL Query
    // Hence, we call the toList method of rowSet to get this value
    identityAPI.addRole(rowSet.toList("NAME").get(i));
  } catch(Exception E) {
    // The Exception may be caused due to the same role being added twice
    // We don't catch any exception here, but it is generally recommended
  }
  i=i+1;
}
try {
  identityAPI.addGroup("ticketingworkflow", "Ticketing Workflow",
    "This is the group for the application Ticketing Workflow",
    null);
} catch (Exception E) {
}
```

Here, we get the identity API from the `apiAccessor` method. This API has the method to add a role based on a name. We iterate through the values of `rowSet`, which contains all the role names, and we keep adding these roles via the identity API. Thus, at the end of this connector, we would have added all the roles returned by the SQL query into our Bonita database. In addition, we are also adding a group called `ticketingworkflow`. We are doing this just to group all the users under multiple roles into a single group.

In the next step, we have to add users to the database. Now, there are specific pieces of information related to every user, such as his/her role and group and also his/her user information. Let us assume that we have all the necessary information in three tables in our database, called `users`, `role`, and `user_role_mapper`. The users table has information such as `user_id`, `username`, `first name`, and `last name`, and the role table has information such as `role_name` and `description`. The `user_role_mapper` table maps users to their roles.

Deploying Bonita on a Server

Now create a connector in the next service step and insert the following SQL query:

```
Select
u.username as USERNAME, u.password as PASSWORD, u.firstname as
   FIRSTNAME,
u.lastname as LASTNAME,  u.email as EMAIL, r.name as NAME
from TICKETING_WORKFLOW.user_role ur
join TICKETING_WORKFLOW.users u on ur.user_id= u.user_id
join TICKETING_WORKFLOW.role r on ur.role_id = r.role_id
```

Thus, we get all the required fields using this SQL query. Now, in the next step of the connector, we need to save the connector output. Here, let us enter the following code in the Groovy editor:

```
import org.ow2.bonita.facade.IdentityAPI;
import org.ow2.bonita.facade.identity.Group;
import org.ow2.bonita.facade.identity.Membership;
import org.ow2.bonita.facade.identity.Role;
import org.ow2.bonita.facade.identity.User;
import org.ow2.bonita.facade.exception.UserAlreadyExistsException

IdentityAPI identityAPI = apiAccessor.getIdentityAPI();

// getGroupUsingPath method expects a list of String
ArrayList<String> groupList = new ArrayList<String>();
list.add("ticketingworkflow");
i=0;
rowSet.getValues().each {
  if(rowSet.toList("USERNAME").get(i)!=null) {
    try {
      User user;
      // We try to add the user, but if the user already exists, then
in the catch block, we just find the user
      try {
        // We give the default password as bpm. The individual users
can change their passwords later on
        user =
          identityAPI.addUser(rowSet.toList("USERNAME").get(i),
          "bpm", rowSet.toList("FIRSTNAME").get(i),
          rowSet.toList("LASTNAME")
          .get(i), rowSet.toList("EMAIL"));
      } catch (UserAlreadyExistsException e) {
        user =
          identityAPI.findUserByUserName(rowSet.toList
          ("USERNAME"));
```

```
        }
        Role role =
           identityAPI.findRoleByName(rowSet.toList("NAME").get(i));
        Group group = identityAPI.getGroupUsingPath(groupList);
        // We define a membership with a specific role and group
        Membership membership =
           identityAPI.getMembershipForRoleAndGroup
           (role.getUUID(),group.getUUID());
        identityAPI.addMembershipToUser
           (user.getUUID(),membership.getUUID());
      } catch (Exception e) {
      }
    }
  }
  i=i+1;
}
```

We have to package the entire process diagram into a business archive file for Bonita Execution Engine to run the workflow. You can export both the process definition and the Web application in a single BAR (Business Archive) file. After exporting the bar file, we can install it using the User Experience. Refer to *Chapter 1, Installing and Getting Started with Bonita* for knowing how to install BAR files. Click on the menu item **Process** and select **Export**. Choose the folder you want the BAR file to be created in and click on **OK**. We've already seen how to install a process in *Chapter 1, Installing and Getting Started with Bonita* through the administrative view.

Thus, we have seen how to deploy Bonita Open Solution on a Tomcat server. The other parameters can be tweaked and played around with for optimal performance and troubleshooting. We can also host external applications on the same Tomcat server and use the redirect to external URL option inside Bonita Studio instead of the inbuilt web form. Thus, we can customize things according to our need.

Summary

In this section, we have learned how to deploy Bonita Open Solution on a Tomcat server, how to customize the database used, and to tweak certain parameters of the Tomcat server to optimize performance. In addition, we have had a look at using the Bonita APIs to make life simpler. As we have seen throughout the book, Bonita Open Solution is a powerful tool for Business Process Modelling and creating swell applications out of it. It is comprehensive software with a powerful engine and a lot of customization options available to make sure that everyone can make use of this tool to solve complex problem statements.

Index

A

admin view 17-19
Alfresco connectors 72
AND gate 58
attachment variable 25, 26

B

Binary Large Object (BLOB) 25
bin folder 112
Bonita API
  about 119-123
  URL, for documentation 119
  users, adding to database 119-123
Bonita BPM 7
Bonita connectors 72-77
Bonita Execution Engine 111
bonita folder 112
Bonita log 117
Bonita Open Solution
  downloading 8
  installing 8
  launching 8
  login page 118
Bonita Open Solution 5.10 8, 111
Bonita Open Solution Community Edition 8
Bonitasoft Community Edition 55, 56
Bonita Studio
  button 30, 31
  connectors 71
  date-picker widget 33
  external form, creating 96, 97
  Image widget 37-39
  inbox view 90-92
  input widget 29, 30
  Message widget 39-47
  Next buttons 47-49
  output widget 29, 30
  Previous buttons 47-49
  process, creating 8-10
  Radio widget 32, 33
  Select widget 32
  User Experience look n feel, creating 106-108
  User XP, customizing 94, 95
  variable 21
  variable, creating 34-37
  web form, creating 29
  web form, customizing 29
  web form, externalizing 96, 97
Bonita Studio Subscription Pack version 52
Boolean variable 24
button 30, 31

C

call activity 63-65
case 11
CMIS connectors 72
conditions
  about 51, 52
  defining, on transitions 56
  evaluating 52
conf folder 112
configuration file
  modifying 117
connectors
  about 71
  groovy scripting connector 85
  types 71-74

URL 85
connectors, types
  Bonita connectors 74-77
  Database connectors 83-85
  Drools connectors 80-83
  e-mail connectors 78-80
contingency 52-55

D

Dashboard 17
database connection
  customizing 114-116
Database connectors 72, 83-85
data, web form
  finalizing 86, 87
date-picker widget 33
date variable 24, 25
DRL file 81
Drools connectors 72, 80-83

E

e-mail connectors
  about 78-80
  configuring 78-80
Entry page flow
  configuring 92, 93
Exchange connectors 72
eXo connectors 72
external folder 112
external form
  creating 96, 97

F

float variable 24

G

Gates 57-59
Gates, types
  AND gate 58
  Inclusive gateway 58
  XOR gate 57
Google connectors 72

Groovy
  URL 52
groovy scripting connector 85

H

human task
  creating 10, 11

I

Image widget 37-39
inbox view 90-92
Inclusive gateway 58
input widget
  creating 29, 30
installation, Bonita Open Solution 8
integer variable 24

J

Jasper connectors 72
Java Authentication and Authorization
      Service (JAAS) 112
Java connectors 72
JavaScript
  alternative to contingency 55, 56
Java variable 26-28
Java Virtual Machine (JVM) 112
JDK
  URL, for downloading 8

L

labels 16
LDAP connectors 72
lib folder 112
logfiles 116, 117
logfiles, types
  Bonita log 117
  Tomcat log 116
login page, Bonita Open Solution 118
logs folder 112
look n feel resource
  creating 103-106
  editing 103-106

modifying 101, 102
template 102

M

message passing event
  about 59-63
  creating 59-63
Message widget 39-47
Messaging connectors 72
multi instantiation 65-70
MySQL Connector 5.0.8
  URL, for downloading 115

N

Next button 47-49

O

output widget
  creating 29, 30
Overview page flow
  configuring 92, 93

P

pool variable
  about 21
  creating 39
  vs, step variable 21
Previous button 47-49
process
  admin view 17-19
  creating 8-10
  Dashboard 17
  human task, creating 10, 11
  labels 16
  running 11-13
  text variable 11
  user inbox 13-15
process history 15, 16
process status, User XP 96

R

Radio widget 32, 33

resources
  adding, to workflow 102, 103

S

Salesforce connectors 72
SAP connectors 72
Scripting connectors 72
Select widget 32
Selenium
  URL 55
Sharepoint connectors 72
Sheetster connectors 72
Social connectors 72
step variable
  about 21
  vs, pool variable 21
SugarCRM connectors 72

T

Talend connectors 72
temp folder 112
text variable 11, 22
Tomcat
  shutting 112, 113
  starting 112, 113
Tomcat 6.0.35 bundle 111
Tomcat bundle
  downloading 111
  exploring 112
  URL, for downloading 111
Tomcat log 116
transitions
  conditions, defining on 56

U

User Experience look n feel
  creating 106-108
user inbox 13-15
users
  adding, to database 119-123
User XP
  customizing 94, 95
  process status 96

V

variable
  creating 34-37
  scope 21
  types 21
variable, types
  attachment variable 25, 26
  Boolean variable 24
  date variable 24, 25
  float variable 24
  integer variable 24
  Java variable 26-28
  pool variable 21
  step variable 21
  text variable 22
View page flow
  configuring 92, 93

W

webapps directory 112
web form
  creating 29
  customizing 29, 99, 100
  data, finalizing 86, 87
  look n feel resource, creating for 103-106
  resources adding, to workflow 102, 103
Web Services connectors 72
work directory 112

X

XOR gate 57
XWiki connectors 72

Thank you for buying
Bonita Open Solution 5.x Essentials

About Packt Publishing
Packt, pronounced 'packed', published its first book "*Mastering phpMyAdmin for Effective MySQL Management*" in April 2004 and subsequently continued to specialize in publishing highly focused books on specific technologies and solutions.

Our books and publications share the experiences of your fellow IT professionals in adapting and customizing today's systems, applications, and frameworks. Our solution based books give you the knowledge and power to customize the software and technologies you're using to get the job done. Packt books are more specific and less general than the IT books you have seen in the past. Our unique business model allows us to bring you more focused information, giving you more of what you need to know, and less of what you don't.

Packt is a modern, yet unique publishing company, which focuses on producing quality, cutting-edge books for communities of developers, administrators, and newbies alike. For more information, please visit our website: www.packtpub.com.

About Packt Open Source
In 2010, Packt launched two new brands, Packt Open Source and Packt Enterprise, in order to continue its focus on specialization. This book is part of the Packt Open Source brand, home to books published on software built around Open Source licences, and offering information to anybody from advanced developers to budding web designers. The Open Source brand also runs Packt's Open Source Royalty Scheme, by which Packt gives a royalty to each Open Source project about whose software a book is sold.

Writing for Packt
We welcome all inquiries from people who are interested in authoring. Book proposals should be sent to author@packtpub.com. If your book idea is still at an early stage and you would like to discuss it first before writing a formal book proposal, contact us; one of our commissioning editors will get in touch with you.

We're not just looking for published authors; if you have strong technical skills but no writing experience, our experienced editors can help you develop a writing career, or simply get some additional reward for your expertise.

Instant Oracle BPM for Financial Services How-to

ISBN: 978-1-782170-14-3　　　Paperback: 62 pages

Discover how to leverage BPM in the financial sector

1. Learn something new in an Instant! A short, fast, focused guide delivering immediate results
2. Simplifies complex business problems for financial services
3. Optimize, enhance, and modify your business processes

Oracle BPM Suite 11g Developer's Cookbook

ISBN: 978-1-849684-22-4　　　Paperback: 512 pages

Over 80 advanced recipes to develop rich, interactive business processes using the Oracle Business Process Management Suite

1. Full of illustrations, diagrams, and tips with clear step-by-step instructions and real time examples to develop Industry Sample BPM Process and BPM interaction with SOA Components
2. Dive into lessons on Fault ,Performance and Rum Time Management
3. Explore User Interaction ,Deployment and Monitoring

Please check **www.PacktPub.com** for information on our titles

[PACKT] open source
community experience distilled

PUBLISHING

Oracle BPM Suite 11g: Advanced BPMN Topics

ISBN: 978-1-849687-56-0　　　Paperback: 114 pages

Master advanced BPMN for Oracle BPM Suite including inter-process communication, handling arrays, and exception management

1. Cover some of the most commonly misunderstood areas of BPMN

2. Gain the knowledge to write professional BPMN processes

3. A practical and concise tutorial packed with advanced topics which until now had received little or no documentation for BPM Suite developers and architects

Instant BlueStacks

ISBN: 978-1-783559-42-8　　　Paperback: 44 pages

Start running Android apps on a Mac/PC in no time using BlueStacks

1. Learn something new in an Instant! A short, fast, focused guide delivering immediate results

2. Learn how to synchronize apps between an Android device and BlueStacks

3. Discover how to install apps from outside the app stores

Please check **www.PacktPub.com** for information on our titles

Printed in Germany
by Amazon Distribution
GmbH, Leipzig